Tales of Ming Emperors and Empresses

– The Thirteen Tombs

Foreign Languages Press

Planned and initiated by: Lan Peijin
Written by: Wei Yuqing
Photographs by: Zhu Li and others
English translation by: Tang Bowen
Designed by: Yuan Qing and others.
Edited by: Lan Peijin

Fist Edition 2007

Tales of Ming Emperors and Empresses
– The Thirteen Tombs

ISBN 978-7-119-05114-7

Published by Foreign Languages Press
24 Baiwanzhuang Road, Beijing 100037, China
Home Page: http://www.flp.com.cn
E-mail Addresses: info@flp.com.cn
                  sales@flp.com.cn

Distributed by China International Book Trading Corporation
35 Chegongzhuang Xilu, Beijing 100044, China
P.O. Box 399, Beijing, China
Printed in the People's Republic of China

Contents

to the Emperor; Court Physicians Swallow Medicine Before the Emperor.

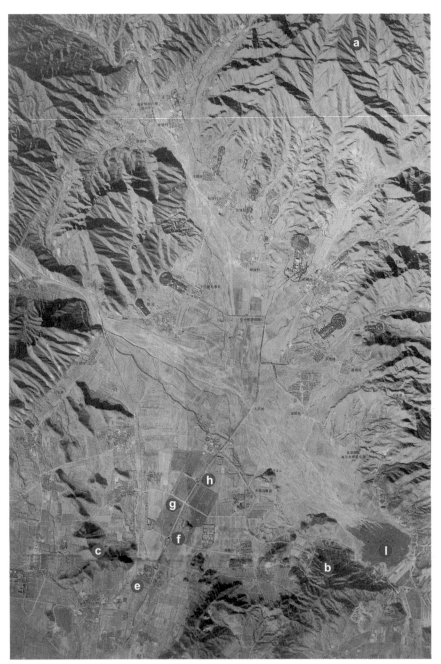

A satellite photo of the Thirteen Tombs area.

The Thirteen Tombs

A Changling
B Xianling
C Jingling
D Yuling
E Maoling
F Tailing
G Kangling
H Yongling
I Zhaoling
J Dingling
K Qingling
L Deling
M Siling

ⓐ Heavenly Longevity Mountain
ⓑ Dragon Mountain
ⓒ Tiger Mountain
ⓓ Stone Arch
ⓔ Great Palace Gate
ⓕ Stele Pavilion
ⓖ Divine Path
ⓗ Flaming Arch
ⓘ Travel Lodge
ⓙ East Well
ⓚ West Well
ⓛ Thirteen Tombs Reservoir

Emperors of the Ming Dynasty

Name	Title of Reign	Years of Reign	Dynastic Title	Tomb
Zhu Yuanzhang	Hongwu	1368−1398 (31)	Taizu	
Zhu Yunwen	Jianwen	1398−1402 (4)	Huidi	
Zhu Di	Yongle	1402−1424 (22)	Chengzu	Changling
Zhu Gaozhi	Hongxi	1424−1425 (1)	Renzong	Xianling
Zhu Zhanji	Xuande	1425−1435 (10)	Xuanzong	Jingling
Zhu Qizhen	Zhengtong	1435−1449 (14)	Yingzong	Yuling
Zhu Qiyu	Jingtai	1449−1457 (8)	Daizong	
Zhu Qizhen	Tianshun	1457−1464 (8)	Yingong	
Zhu Jianshen	Chenghua	1464−1487 (23)	Xianzong	Maoling
Zhu Youcheng	Hongzhi	1487−1505 (18)	Xiaozong	Tailing
Zhu Houzhao	Zhengde	1505−1521 (16)	Wuzong	Kangling
Zhu Houcong	Jiajing	1521−1566 (45)	Shizong	Yongling
Zhu Zaihou	Longqing	1566−1572 (6)	Muzong	Zhaoling
Zhu Yijun	Wanli	1572−1620 (48)	Shenzong	Dingling
Zhu Changluo	Taichang	1620 (1)	Guangzong	Qingling
Zhu Youjiao	Tianqi	1620−1627 (7)	Xizong	Deling
Zhu Youjian	Chongzhen	1627−1644 (17)	Sizong	Siling

The Thirteen Tombs

Where Do the Emperors and Empresses Go When They Die? In the Underground "Forbidden City" They Gather.

The Thirteen Tombs is the popular name of the tombs where thirteen emperors of the Ming dynasty were buried. The tombs are located in a broad basin surrounded by mountain ridges on three sides in Changping District, some 40 kilometers from Beijing city centre. In the north are the main peaks of the Heavenly Longevity Mountain, which "look like ten thousand horses galloping down from heaven." The

Stone arch glorifying the virtue and exploits of ancestors.

Great Palace Gate, the main entrance to the tombs area.

Dragon and Tiger mountains on the eastern and western sides are like a dragon and a tiger guarding the entrance to the basin. The Wenyu River winds its way from the northwest through the basin. In terms of geomantic quality, the location "guarded by mountains, with a river flowing through it, sheltered against wind and good for amassing the vital energy," is believed to be one that promises good fortune.

After mounting the throne in Nanjing in 1402, Zhu Di, the third emperor of the Ming dynasty, was faced with the question of national security. The Yuan dynasty of the Mongols was overthrown, but its remnant forces were still entrenched in the north and must be seriously dealt with by the Ming government. As soon as he became the emperor, Zhu Di decided to move the capital from Nanjing in the south to Beijing and began to build his palace and his future tomb, known as Changling, there. Following his example, the Ming emperors who came after him also built their tombs in the area. After more than 230 years, from 1409 to 1644, the tombs eventually were scattered over an area of 40 square kilometers, turning the basin into "a holy area of imperial tombs."

To facilitate administration and the performance of sacrificial ceremonies, there were a Thanks-giving Hall and a

Dismounting Stone.

Clothes and Gear Hall in the tomb area for the emperor to rest and change, a Fasting House for officials, a Work Department for maintenance of the tombs, living quarters for eunuchs of the Tomb Administration Department, a slaughtering pavilion for sacrificial animals, a kitchen and orchards. In addition to the stone markers erected around the tomb area warning intruders, there were border walls and 10 watch towers at the mountain passes, where guards were stationed. According to written records, the guards at the tombs totaled more than 37,600 men during the middle period of the Ming dynasty. Removing soil, quarrying and felling trees for making charcoal were strictly forbidden. Violators were punishable by exile and even by death.

Throughout history, the tombs of emperors were regarded as symbols of the state and always given special importance and protection.

The Main Gate to the tomb area, popularly known as the Great Palace Gate, was built on an elevated ground between the mountains on the eastern and western sides. The gate tower was an imposing structure of red walls and yellow glazed

Stele Pavilion.

roof tiles. The tall and thick walls on either side of the gate extended to the top of the mountains on the eastern and western sides like the Great Wall. What we can see today are only ruins of the walls. The gate was closed on ordinary days. Attendants to the tombs used the two side gates.

Stone kylin unicorn.

Following traditional customs, several sacrificial ceremonies were performed every year in the tomb area. There were three major sacrificial ceremonies (on the Clear and Bright Festival, Festival of the Dead Spirits and Winter Solstice) and four minor sacrificial ceremonies (on the anniversary of the emperor's death, birthday of the Water God, the emperor's birthday and early winter). Activities included burning incense, performing sacrificial rituals and delivering elegiac addresses.

Stone lion.

Divine Path.

Stone horse.

Stone elephant.

Stone Xiezhi, a fabulous animal.

The memorial ceremonies for the anniversaries of death of the emperors and empresses were held individually at the respective tombs. On the Clear and Bright Festival when flowers were in full bloom in spring, the emperor living in the palace often brought his empress and imperial concubines to the tombs to offer sacrifices and also took the opportunity to enjoy spring in the countryside. It was usually a grand occasion participated by as many as 10,000 people, including palace maids, eunuchs, accompanying officials, guards and laborers. The usually quiet tomb area was turned into a noisy place.

In front of the Great Palace Gate is a broad square. A memorial archway of green stone stands not far to the south of the square. This structure of five passages and six columns that stands across the main path is 14 meters high and nearly 30 meters wide and built in the style of a wooden structure. It was constructed in 1540 by the 11th emperor of the Ming dynasty to extol the exploits of his ancestors. There are no inscriptions on any part of the archway, but the carved decorations were exquisitely executed with dragons in clouds and lively lions.

There is a stone tablet at both the eastern and western sides of the square inscribed with the words: "Officials and others are to dismount here." Known as Dismounting Stones, they order people to come down from their horses and car-

Stone warrior.

riages to show respects for the ancestors.

In the tomb area, a main path leading to the individual tombs is known as the Divine Path, because it was the path along which the souls of the emperors and empresses were believed to go the their places of eternal rest. Near the start of the path is a square pavilion with a stone stele of 6.5 meters in height in it. The front side of the stele is inscribed with more than 3,000 words written by Zhu Gaozhi, the fourth emperor of the Ming dynasty, recording the accomplishments of his father, Zhu Di, the third emperor. Because Zhu Gaozhi died of illness less than a year after he was in the throne, the inscription was not carved on the stele until 10 years later in 1435.

Not far from the four corners of the Stele Pavilion are four ornamental marble columns, each carved with

Stone senior official.

Stone civil official.

a dragon winding around the column and rising to the sky among clouds. At the top of each of the columns is a strange beast known as Sky-watching Beast, howling in the direction of or away from the imperial palace. It is said that the beast howling in the direction of the palace is urging the emperor to come out of the palace to look into the life of the ordinary people, and the one howling away from the palace is calling the emperor to come back to the palace to handle state affairs.

Standing on either side of the path north of the pavilion are 18 pairs of stone human figures and beasts representing the honor guard for the emperor when he came out. This tradition of lining stone figures in front of a tomb started 2,000 years ago during the Qin and Han dynasties.

Among the carved stone figures and beasts, the fabulous animal known as Xiezhi is the most interesting. It is said that it is able to distinguish between evil and good and uses its single horn to stab "evil persons." Its image was embroidered on the hat

Flaming Arch at the end of the Divine Path.

Immortal's Cave.

and robe of the law officials of the Ming dynasty to indicate honesty and uprightness.

The stone figures of civil and military officials are also finely and lively carved. They are highly valuable for the study of the clothes and ornaments worn by officials of the Ming dynasty.

At the end of the Divine Path is an exquisitely constructed archway of stone and bricks. Known as the Dragon and Phoenix Gate or the Flaming Archway, it was built in the style of the Gate to Heaven as people imagined it. After passing this gate, the souls of the emperors and empresses were believed to be able to reach directly to heaven, a quiet and peaceful place totally free from worries.

Encircling wall of the tombs area.

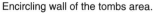

Changling

Zhu Di, Emperor Chengzu.

Changling, the tomb of Zhu Di, the third emperor of the Ming dynasty, and his Empress Xu, is the first and the largest of the Thirteen Tombs. Built between 1409 and 1427 and occupying about 120,000 square meters of grounds, it is located at the center of the tomb area. The entire tomb is modeled on the imperial palace, complete with the front hall and the rear sleeping hall. The front part, rectangular in shape, with the main hall and side buildings in it is supposed to

A bird's-eye view of Changling.

be the emperor's work place. The circular rear part with coffins in an underground palace below an earth mound is the living area of the emperor and empress. (Some people say that the design is based on the ancient philosophical idea that the earth is square and heaven round.) Symmetry was always emphasized in ancient Chinese architecture. All the main structures were arranged along an axis.

The Lingen Hall is the main surface building of the emperor's tomb, where things, clothes, armor and weapons used by the emperor were stored and looked after by eunuchs. The hall was also the place for holding memorial ceremonies. Its importance was just like the Hall of Supreme Harmony among the three main halls in the imperial palace. As it was the highest in rank among the imperial structures, it is a building of nine bays with double eaves and a hipped roof.

Completed in 1427, the Lingen Hall is the largest and the most imposing hall built of *nanmu* wood still

The main gate of Changling.

extant in China. The roof of the hall is supported by 60 huge *nanmu* columns, the largest of which measures 1.17 meters in diameter and over 14 meters high. The hall is immensely precious because it is the only one of its kind among ancient structures.

The Prince of Yan Builds Up a Big Army; A War Breaks Out Between Uncle and Nephew.

After overthrowing the rule of the Yuan dynasty at the head of an insurgent army, Zhu Yuanzhang, of peasant origin, ascended to the throne in Nanjing and founded the Great Ming dynasty. Intending to keep imperial power for ever in the hands of the Zhu family, he followed the rule of "appointing the eldest son as the heir apparent" and made him the crown prince.

Lingen Gate.

He also ennobled his 23 other sons and stationed them in the various parts of the country as princes.

Although the Yuan emperor and his empresses and followers had been driven to the north of the deserts at the time, he still commanded an army of considerable size and often harassed areas south of the Great Wall. Faced with this situation, Zhu appointed several of the princes as frontier princes in command of powerful armies. Zhu Di, the Prince of Yan and his fourth son, was one of the frontier princes.

Conferred the title of the Prince of Yan at 11, Zhu Di (1360-1424) moved to his fiefdom in Beiping (Beijing), or Khanbalig, the former capital of the Yuan dynasty, when his was 20. While in Beiping, he led his army several times to the north of the Great Wall and displayed unusual military talent by winning many victories. During his northern expeditions, Zhu Di not only multiplied the heavy weapons and horses of his army, but also increased the strength of his army by recruiting many Mogol cavalrymen into his army.

In 1392, when the kindhearted crown prince Zhu Biao died of illness, it was said that Zhu Yuanzhang intended to make the Prince of Yan his crown prince, but several senior court officials advised against it. He appointed instead his eldest grandson, Zhu Yunwen, as the crown prince. In his later years, Zhu Yuanzhang instructed the Prince of Yan on several occasions "to control his army and act as a leader of the princes." He hoped that this son of his would do all he could to assist Zhu Yunwen in succeeding to the throne and in the smooth transition of power in the Zhu family.

In 1398, after the death of Zhu Yuanzhang at the age of 71, his 21-year-old grandson succeeded to the throne and became known in history as Emperor Jianwen. As soon as he became the emperor, he was most uneasy because his uncles who had been enfeoffed in various parts of the country were all in command of powerful armies. He called together several of his ministers at the eastern corner gate of the palace to discuss ways of dealing with the situation. Two of the ministers, Qi Tai and Huang Zicheng, suggested that the emperor should follow the example of Emperor Jingdi of the Han dynasty (reigning 156-141 B.C.), take power back from the princes, transfer them to other places and reduce the number of their followers. Following their advice, Zhu Yunwen immediately went into action. According history books, two months after ascending to the throne, he dealt with several frontier princes, either stripping them of their titles, reducing them to commoners or condemning them to life imprisonment or death.

In July 1399, the Prince of Yan received an important intelligence report, which informed him that Emperor Jianwen was about to take action against him. After scheming secretly with his confidants, he lured the officials sent by the court to Beiping to a banquet in the prince's mansion and had them killed. He then started a revolt in the name of an expeditionary war to "purge bad elements from among the aides to the emperor." This became known in history as "the War of Pacification." Only a year after the death of Zhu Yuanzhang, the Prince of Yan, who was supposed to assist the Ming court, became the leader in usurping the throne. The war lasted four years. In 1402, Nanjing was taken by the army of the Prince of Yan. It was said that the palace was engulfed in a huge fire. Both Zhu Yunwen and his empress were burned to death. As their faces had become hardly distinguishable, sev-

Carved stones on the steps.

eral corpses were collected together and hastily buried. The whereabouts of Zhu Yunwen has eventually become a great mystery in the history of the Ming dynasty.

The Ruthless One Wins in a Fratricidal Strife; Many Are the Innocents Killed by Sword and Arrow.

"The War of Pacification" that lasted more than four years was a very difficult one. As it is commonly said: "It requires blood brothers fighting together to kill a tiger, and father and son in an army to win victory." Blood relationship becomes highly important at crucial moments. In this war, Zhu Di was assisted by Zhu Gaoxi, his second son. Described in history books as "a ferocious person and a good horseman and archer," Zhu Gaoxi was a highly competent general on the battlefield. As Zhu Di, the Prince of Yan, was always at the head of his army in making charges, it was said that once after his horse was

wounded in a battle, he was surrounded by the enemy. It was Zhu Gaoxi who rushed to the cordon and saved his father. As a result, the Prince of Yan showed even greater favor to this son of his.

On the other hand, Zhu Yunwen, or Emperor Jianwen, was handicapped by consideration for the blood relationship between uncle and nephew. He repeatedly

Name sign of Lingen Gate.

ordered his army not to harm his uncle. Taking advantage of his nephew's weakness, Zhu Di fought and killed ruthlessly from the start and eventually defeated his nephew.

Prompted by many of his close followers, Zhu Di took the throne four days after occupying Nanjing, changing the reigning title to Yongle and becoming known in history as Emperor Yongle when he was 42. The legitimacy of Zhu Di's assumption of the throne gave rise to a great debate in Nanjing at the time. As most of the officials of Emperor Jianwen's court were against it, this resulted in a massive, indiscriminate killing known as the "Implication Incident." Even the family and clan members of the officials who refused to tot the line were involved. As many as more than 10,000 people were said to have been killed.

Zhu Di was also ruthless towards the family members of Emperor Jianwen. Two of Emperor Jianwen's

Lingen Hall.

three younger brothers were locked up until they died in prison. The third 16-year-old younger brother was ordered to look after the grave of Emperor Jianwen and was later burned to death in his house. Emperor Jianwen had two sons. The seven-year-old elder son became lost after the fall of Nanjing. The two-year-old second son, Zhu Wengui, was locked up in the Zhu family's home town in Fengyang, Anhui. It was not until more than 50 years later that Zhu Qizhen, the sixth emperor of the Ming dynasty, suddenly called to mind the existence of the second son. He sent a eunuch to deal with him. When the second son walked out of the prison, he could not even tell the difference between a horse and a cow. It was a heartrending sight.

Zhu Di was said to have become conscience-smitten later for the excessive killing. He had a large bronze bell cast in Beijing (known as the Yongle Bell) with Buddhist scriptures carved on it to redeem the lost souls of the innocents. Later historians were justified to judge this part of Zhu Di's life as being characterized by excessively severe punishments and excessive killing.

Disturbances Arise on the Northern Frontier; A Tomb Is Built Before Moving the Capital.

After assuming the throne in Nanjing, Zhu Di's main attention was on the defense of the northern frontier. This was because the Mongols north of the desert still had a strong army. He was also haunted

Lingen Hall is supported by 60 columns of costly nanmu wood, each nearly 12 meters high and 1.17 meters in diameter.

Flaming Gate.

by doubts about the disappearance of Emperor Jianwen. This made him think of moving the capital. Beijing had been his old base where he had worked for more than 20 years. As there were not only his men, but also his administrative structures there, he was thoroughly familiar with the place and the people there. In his second year in the throne (1403), he decreed that the name of Beiping be changed into Beijing and set up the six boards of administration. From then on, he stayed most of the time in Beijing, which had become the de facto capital.

In the early period of the Ming dynasty, Zhu Yuanzhang had ordered the demolition of the Yuan palace in Khanbalig. Taking the opportunity of moving the capital, Zhu Di decided to rebuild the palace in Beijing. A number of officials were sent out in the fourth year of Yongle (1406) to various places in the country to collect the necessary materials, such as wood, stone and bricks. It was an arduous task. Lumbermen had to work throughout the year deep in the mountain forests in Hunan and Sichuan to look for suitable giant trees. A history book says, "Of 1,000 men working in the mountains, only 500 came out."

In 1407, Empress Xu, who was two years younger, died of illness in Nanjing when she was only 46 years old. The eldest daughter of General Xu Da, who helped in the founding of the Ming dynasty, she was married to the Prince of Yan at 15 and had given birth to three sons and two daughters. A competent woman and wife, she managed to keep the rear quarters of the imperial palace in perfect order. According to traditional customs, the empress and emperor were to be buried together when they died and their tomb would become a symbol of the ancestral foundation. Since Zhu Di had decided to move the capital to Beijing, her tomb was to be built there. When she died, she was interned in Nanjing and officials were sent to Beijing to look for an "auspicious site" for the construction of her tomb.

After the officials had chosen the site, Zhu Di came in person to see it and was highly satisfied with it. Construction of the tomb began after a ceremony of offering sacrifices to Heaven and Earth. The hill behind the tomb was renamed the Heavenly Longevity Mountain. When the gigantic underground palace was completed in 1413, Empress Xu's coffin was taken to Beijing and entombed in it. This tomb in Changping was called Changling. As all the building materials, military and civil workers and craftsmen were transferred from the construction sites of the future imperial palace in the city of Beijing, the construction of the palace did not start in full scale until the empress

Surface structures of Changling.

was entombed.

The new palace in Beijing was modeled on the old palace in Nanjing but was far more grandeur and magnificent. The palace alone was comprised of more than 1,630 rooms. If the mansion of the crown prince and mansions for other princes outside the Eastern Peace Gate were included, there were altogether 8,350 rooms. Since the overall architectural arrangement of the palace emphasized imperial authority and since the layout of the city of Beijing also aimed at meeting that need, the layout of the city of Beijing had remained basically unchanged during the 500 and more years of the Ming and Qing dynasties.

When the construction in Beijing was basically completed in the 18th year of Yongle (1420), Zhu Di announced to the world that beginning from the 19th year of Yongle, the capital was formally moved from Nanjing to Beijing.

Sailing to the Western Ocean to Show Power and Good Will; No Traces of the Missing Emperor Jianwen Can Be Found.

Historians have made many favorable comments on the historical roles played by Zhu Di. One of the roles he played was sending a large fleet to countries in Southeast Asia, known as "Zheng He sailing to the western ocean" in history. The ships in which Zheng He sailed measured over 142 meters long and 57.6 meters wide and as high as a building of many stories. As about 28,000 men sailed together in each of the trips, each of the ships had a capacity for about 450 men. When this huge fleet with tens of thousands of soldiers on it dropped anchor at the ports of various countries along the route, it displayed the power and good will of the Great Ming Empire. But carrying on trade and strengthening friendly contact was still the main purpose of the visits of the fleet.

Beginning from 1405, Zheng He sailed seven times to countries in Southeast Asia and reached as far as Somalia on the eastern African coast. The fleet carried silk fabrics, tea, porcelain ware, iron goods and things for everyday life. Part of the things were given as gifts to kings and tribal chiefs along the way. The rest was for trade or exchange for local products, such as spices, medicines, pearls and jewels, rare birds and animals. History books recorded that the Smalt blue pigment for making the famous blue-and-white porcelain of the Ming dynasty was imported for Indonesia. The precious emerald worn by high officials and rich women was from Aden on the Arabian Peninsula. The visits of the fleet also brought back to China princes and other relatives sent by many of the kings and chieftains along the route to visit China. These princes and relatives brought back many pleasant memories with them for the later people.

It was said that a secret objective of Zheng He's sailing overseas was to continue the search for the missing Emperor Jianwen. After taking the throne, a rumor spread far and wide among the people, saying that Emperor Jianwen had made his escape from the palace and had become a monk and sailed overseas. Disquieted by the rumor, Zhu Di sent men all over the country to search for the lost emperor in the temples and monasteries. As this coincided with Zheng He's sailing overseas, it was reasonable for Zhu Di to entrust Zheng with the task of searching for Emperor

Jianwen overseas. The task was not fulfilled because there is no mention of it in history books. It should be a historical fact that the disappearance of Emperor Jianwen mentally disturbed Zhu Di all his life.

The Emperor Leads Punitive Expeditions; He Dies of Illness at Yumuchuan.

After becoming the emperor, Zhu Di took many measures to stabilize the northern frontiers. In addition to stationing armies over an extensive area and strengthening the defense of the frontier towns, he adopted a policy of appeasement towards the leaders of various ethnic groups by assigning them to official posts and conferring titles on them. He also vigorously promoted trade by barter to facilitate peaceful contact between peoples. But there were still some powerful tribal leaders who often took advantage of the harvest time in autumn to make long-distance raids on horseback, crossed the Great Wall and passes to harass the farming areas on the plains. In order to find out the real situation on the frontier and make correct decisions or even for the purpose of training his army and raising its combat effectiveness, Zhu Di led in person five expeditions to the north

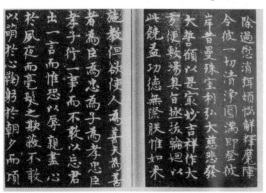

Inscription in Zhu Di's handwriting.

while he was in the throne. As an army of several hundred thousand was mobilized each time, the expeditions played a deterring role. Upon hearing the news of the expedition, the local chieftains either ran away or bowed down in submission. The army of the Great Ming Empire naturally returned in triumph. This was followed by the army's triumphant entry into the city of Beijing through the Victory Gate and jubilant celebrations in the palace. The Ming dynasty was at the height of its power and splendor at the time.

Zhu Di launched his fifth expedition in the early spring of the 22nd year of Yongle (1424). Report reached Beijing that the Mongol chieftain Alutai was about to invade the city of Datong. Although it was less than a year from the last expedition, Zhu Di insisted on personally leading another northern expedition despite advice against it by high court officials. After holding a sacrificial ceremony to Heaven and Earth and an oath-taking rally, he led the army out of the Juyong Pass of the Great Wall on the fourth day of the fourth month and headed north straight for the base of Alutai. When the great army reached Dalanamur River in today's Mongolia in the sixth month, Alutai had already fled farther north. On the boundless desert

Stove for burning elegiac address written on silk.

Portrait of Empress Xu. According to "Notes on Carriages and Clothing" in the *History of the Ming Dynasty*, "The empress's informal wear ... includes a headgear decorated with a golden dragon and two phoenixes, each holding a pearl in its mouth. The front and back are decorated with a peony flower made of strings of pearls. Each flower has eight stamens and 36 green leaves. The side ornaments of three crosses are formed by 24 golden designs and strings of pearls..... The robe is yellow in color and the cloak of dark blue decorated with dragon and cloud designs embroidered in gold....." The two-phoenix and a dragon decoration, three crosses and the colorful cloak and the ample-sleeved robe are in accordance with the specifications for the empress wear laid down in the third year of the Yongle reign.

and vast grassland, there was no sign of any Mongols. At this moment, the Ming army was beset with supply problems. Following the advice by high officials, Zhu Di ordered the return of the army to the capital. But on the way, he fell ill. Although he had counted the days he was to travel before reaching Beijing, he died on the 17th day of the seventh month at a place named Yumuchuan (in Inner Mongolia's Dolundo today) when he was 65.

After the emperor died, the high officials traveling with the army decided to follow the example of the First Emperor of the Qin dynasty who died during his travel away from the capital and not to announce the death immediately. While a confidant was sent back to the capital to report the death of the emperor to the crown prince, all the tin vessels used by the soldiers were collected together, melt and cast into a large box. The emperor's body was placed in the box and loaded onto a large cart shaded from the sun, while "his daily routine was followed just as before." When the crown prince met them at the Juyong Pass, the news of the death of the emperor was formally announced to the world. They reached Beijing on the 18th day of the eighth month. The tunnel leading to the underground palace was opened and Emperor Yongle was entombed in Changling.

Concubines Are Cruelly Buried with the Dead Emperor; The Eastern and Western Wells Are in Ruins

A distance to the left and right in front of Changling in the area of the Thirteen Tombs are some architectural ruins, where the foundations of halls, gates and walls are still discernible. The bases of columns and broken tiles and bricks are scattered in tree shades and among wild grass. These are the places

Crumbling wall of the graveyard at East Well.

where the 16 concubines who were buried after the death of Zhu Di. The two places are known as the Eastern and Western Wells. The word "well" meant deep burial and there are no tunnels leading to them.

After the founding the Great Ming Empire, Zhu Yuanzhang repeatedly declared that he would follow the institutions of the Han and Tang dynasties in ruling the country. But facts show that although he carried on the traditions, he was guilty of retrogression. The burial of living persons with the dead, for example, was abolished more than 1,000 years before him. It was revived in the Ming dynasty. History books recorded that Zhu Yuanzhang was buried with more than 40 court ladies when he died. Although the official history of the Ming dynasty tries purposely to hide the facts or makes only casual mention of them, leaving no complete records of those buried with the dead, many reliable facts have been passed down to the present.

After the death of Zhu Di, the persons and number of the persons to be buried with the dead emperor were to be decided by the new emperor. They were basically concubines who had not given birth to

children. On the day of the burial, these people were taken to a room in a courtyard, where they were given beautiful clothes and nice food and then led by eunuchs to a special room, where they were to stand on a square stool and put their heads into a noose tied on the beam. When the eunuch kicked away to stool, "each of

A stone stele at the graveyard for burying imperial concubines at West Well.

them died by suicide." This is a brief account of their tragic death. History books say that "the sound of wailing shook the halls" at the time.

The burial of living persons continued for four generations of the Ming emperors. It was Zhu Qizhen, the sixth emperor, who was eventually conscience-stricken in 1464 and decreed before his death the cessation of the practice. Only then did the court ladies gradually forget their constant fear and worries because they did not know when they would be buried with the emperor.

Xianling

Xianling

Xianling, built in 1425, is the tomb of Zhu Gaozhi, the fourth Ming emperor, and his wife, Empress Zhang. Since he had instructed before his death that his tomb was to be frugally and simply built, Xianling is comparatively smaller in scale.

The Crown Prince Is Insecure in His Position; Challenge Comes from His Two Brothers.

Zhu Gaozhi (1378-1425), the eldest son of the emperor, was made the crown prince when he was 26 years old. As he was a very fat man with a big paunch, his father, Zhu Di, had repeatedly told him to eat less and reduce his weight, but to no avail. It was also said that he also had two bad legs and had to be helped along to walk. When his father launched the coup d'état, his military performance was far less impressive than his two younger brothers because he was not a good rider and archer. Zhu Di did not place much hope on this successor of his. As the crown prince, he was told to stay in Nanjing all those years.

Zhu Di had more than once intended to replace the crown prince and had discussed it with court officials. During the discussion, one of the officials said that the crown prince was benevolent and exemplary in filial devotion. When the official saw that the emperor was not pleased to hear it, he added that the crown prince's eldest son was an outstanding grandson. This probably made the emperor divert his love for his son to his grandson. He paid close attention to the training of his grandson and took his grandson with him during several of his northern expeditions. There was a painting of a big tiger and a tiger cub preserved in the palace. One day, the emperor asked the court officials to inscribe a poem on it. Making use of the subject of the painting, the officials discussed a moment and wrote: "Where is the man who dares to anger the tiger, the king of all animals? Only the love between father and son makes the tiger turn round to look at the cub repeatedly." The emperor was deeply moved by the inscription. Afterwards, he never mentioned replacing the crown prince again. But the crown prince's two brothers did not behave decently and created many disturbances.

Zhu Gaoxi, the crown prince's first younger brother, was conferred the title of the Prince of Han.

Surface structures at Xianling.

A good rider and archer interested in military strategy, he fought with his father and attained many merits. Zhu Di thought he was very much like himself. Later, accused of secretly and illegally manufacturing weapons and training soldiers, he was punished by being locked at the palace's Western Flowery Gate. After he was made a prince, he should have moved to his fiefdom immediately. But he continued to stay in the capital on various excuses. When the rumor of the replacement of the crown prince became widespread. Zhu Di had no choice but to dispatch him forcibly to his fiefdom in Le'an Prefecture in Shandong.

Zhu Gaosui, the crown prince's second younger brother and the Prince of Zhao, had always lived in the capital and made many sworn friends in and out of the palace and among government officials and military officers. A eunuch named Huang Yan was trusted by Zhu Di and very close to Zhu Gaosui. He informed Zhu Gaosui of many secret events in the palace. Zhu Di suffered from rheumatism in his later years and often left court affairs unattended. As the crown prince was not trusted, Huang Yan thought it was an opportunity to urge the Prince of Zhao to seize the throne and spread rumors saying that Zhu Di was about to pass the throne to the Prince of Zhao. Some military men who were eager for immediate success and gain also wanted to put the Prince of Zhao in the throne through a palace coup. They had even assigned people to steal military tallies and seals from the palace storeroom and to arrest officials who were against the coup.

One day in the fifth month of the 21st year of Yongle (1423), an imperial edict was suddenly issued from the palace imposing a curfew in the whole city and making massive arrests. All those who were involved in the plot were rounded up. The plot failed because a middle-rank officer reported them to the court. Huang Yan and several hundred others were executed. Although the Prince of Zhao was involved, he pretended to know nothing about the plot and refused to answer any questions. When Zhu Di died a year later, the attempted coup was forgotten.

Empress and Concubines Are Long at Odds; A Cup of Wine Heightens the Suspicion.

After ascending to the throne, Zhu Gaozhi at first intended to make progress and do something for the country. He not only appointed virtuous officials, listened to advice with an open mind and acknowledge and correct his mistakes. But this did not last very long. He soon began to indulge in wine and women and became neglectful in state affairs. Some court officials had submitted memorials criticizing him for "indulging in wine and women and not holding court at specified time, so that the large number of officials did not know whether it was to be held in the morning or evening." But Zhu Gaozhi simply ignored the advice of the officials.

During his life, Zhu Gaozhi conferred the titles of empresses and imperial concubines on 11 women, who had given birth to 10 sons and seven daughters. Empress Zhang was a woman of female virtues from a well-to-do scholar's family. Imperial Concubine Guo was the granddaughter of Guo Ying, Marquis of Wuding, an official who had rendered outstanding service for the founding of the dynasty. After coming to the palace, she became arrogant and unreasonable. Other ordinary concubines did not dare to be at odds with her. There was another imperial concubine named Tan, a clever and ingenious woman from a commoner's family well favored by the emperor. These three and the other eight women all lived in the rear quarters of the palace. Although each of them lived in a detached house with a courtyard enclosed by walls, there were always gossips going around to stir up trouble. All the troubles had to be remedied by Empress Zhang as head of the rear quarters before they develop into a disaster.

The seventh day of the fourth month in the first year of Hongxi (1425) was the 46th birthday of Empress Zhang. All the imperial concubines and wives of

Autumn in the tombs area.

the senior officials in the capital had to follow the tradition and come to the palace to congratulate. It was probably because of some old grudges. When Imperial Concubine Guo offered Empress Zhang a cup of wine, the empress stubbornly refused to drink. To gross over the awkward situation, the emperor picked up the cup of wine offered to the empress and drank it. As he drank, he said, "Why are you not drinking the wine Guo offered to you? Are you afraid the wine is poisoned?" What the emperor said did not carry any implications at all, but Guo was terrified. It was said that she committed suicide when she returned to her quarters. The incident became an unsolved case in history, because 34 days later, at dawn on the 11th day of the fifth month, the emperor died. Many people blamed Guo for allowing the emperor to drink the poisoned wine and deduced that she committed suicide because of her poisoned wine. But others disagreed on this conclusion. They questioned why it took a whole month for the poison to take effect and why there were no symptoms before the emperor died. As there were all kinds of deductions, no one could decide which one was correct. Later, a eunuch who was in the know told that the emperor was indeed died of poisoning. But the poison was not in Guo's wine. As the emperor led a life of dissipation, he contracted venereal disease. Eager to cure his disease, he swallowed some metallic and mineral drugs given to him by some quake doctors and was poisoned to death. To cover up this disgraceful affair, it was recorded that the emperor died a natural death.

Jingling

Jingling, built in 1435, is the burial place of Zhu Zhanji, the fifth emperor of the Ming dynasty, and his second empress, Sun. Limited by local terrain, the tomb was elongated in shape. A hundred years later, in 1536, Emperor Jiajing considered that the architectural style of Jingling was not in accord with the exploits of his forefather and ordered its expansion. But the expansion did not alter the overall narrow style of the tomb.

History books say that the structures of Jingling,

A distant view of Jingling.

such as the stone gates, tunnels, well with carved railings, stone beds and sacrificial objects, were copies of those in Changling. The descriptions are believed to be true because of the stabilized social conditions and economic growth at the time.

The Grandfather Goes on an Expedition; He Places His Hope on His Eldest Grandson.

Zhu Zhanji (1399-1435), known as Emperor Xuande in history, was made the heir apparent as the eldest grandson of the emperor when he was 11. This proved that Zhu Di, his grandfather, was disappointed with the crown prince and placed the task of carrying forward the dynastic cause on his grandson. To train his grandson for the throne, he invited a number of learned scholars to give instructions to his grandson on rites, philosophy, poetry and music as well as playing the lute and chess and the art of painting and

Inside Jingling.

calligraphy. As a result, Zhu Zhanji became proficient in writing and painting and, after ascending to the throne, often composed and recited poems and painted pictures with senior court officials. When he had time to spare, he put on armor and led an army of thousands of men to hunt on the grassland outside the Great Wall and practice fighting a battle.

When Zhu Di was alive, every time he went on an expedition to the other side of the Great Wall, he took his grandson with him so that the young man could be familiar with things in the army and the mountains, rivers and geographical conditions of his country. Zhu Di also took him to ordinary people's houses along the way to see what the peasants ate and wore and the farming tools they used, so that he would understand the hardships of the ordinary people. The teachers and court officials who traveled with him gave him detailed lessons on Confucian classics, such as "The people are the foundation; the ruler is less in importance." All the things Zhu Di did embodied the grandfather's hope in his grandson. All this produced certain results in the later days. When Zhu Zhanji was in the throne, he showed concern for the people's livelihood, issued many decrees to distribute relief to people and exempt taxes in disaster-stricken areas. In government affairs, he paid attention to appointing virtuous and competent people and set strict demand on officials close to him. But as years went by, he began to overstep the bounds in his behavior.

Emperor Xuande Indulges in Cricket Fight; The Hobby Becomes Widespread.

When Zhu Zhanji was in the throne, the Ming dynasty was in a period of fast economic growth and stable political situation. The emperor in his thirties was in the most energetic period of his life. As he lived deep in the palace and had not much to do, he thought of various ways of passing his time. Besides practicing calligraphy and painting pictures, he found funs in throwing large handfuls of gold and silver ornaments to the ground for the officials to snatch and in gambling with the eunuchs in dog or cock fights or in the pitch-pot game by throwing arrows into a pot.

One day, Zhu Zhanji saw by chance a group of eunuchs watching a cricket fight. As the wet places at the foot of the palace walls, brick seams and growth

The blank stone stele.

of grass were ideal places for insects to reproduce, their chirping provided good music for the lonely imperial concubines and palace maids in the long autumn nights. As the crickets are bellicose insects, their fights provided amusement for the eunuchs in the palace. Guided by the eunuchs, Zhu Zhanji began to find interest in cricket fights. Catching, selecting, feeding, training the crickets to fight involved a great deal of know-how, which Zhu Zhanji had never heard before and could not be learned from his teachers.

The emperor had to learn from the eunuchs that there were many kinds of crickets of different sizes, color and habits. Since the climatic conditions in the south were more suitable for crickets to grow in size, and the crickets found there were resistant to disease and brave in fighting. When they fought, they never backed out from battle, not even when a leg was bitten off by the opponent. Upon hearing what he was told, Zhu Zhanji sent eunuchs to several places in the south to find the best crickets at whatever prices. Later, it was said that a good cricket cost more than 10 ounces of silver.

In the ninth year of Xuande (1434), Zhu Zhanji even sent a special message to officials in the Suzhou area, ordering them to assist in purchasing crickets. The eunuch sent from Beijing stayed in Suzhou to supervise the buying. When news spread out, people were enticed by the high princes and came out everywhere to try to catch crickets by the rivers and canals, in front and behind houses. The chief of a local grain station was unable to meet his quota for crickets. He had to exchange a fine horse for a qualified cricket. His wife was utterly puzzled and thought the cricket worth the price of a fine horse must be a very unusual one. She opened the jar and wanted to look at it. The cricket jumped out of the jar and disappeared. For fear of being blamed for her blunder, she committed suicide. When the chief of the grain station returned home, he was overcome with grief and killed himself, too. There is a story about crickets in the famous classical novel *Strange Tales from Liaozhai Studio*, which describes a shocking tragedy that befalls on a junior local official's family because of the emperor of the Xuande period favored cricket game.

As cricket fight became widely popular in society, the manufacture of cricket jars developed with it. Jingdezhen was one of the centers for making porcelain articles for the palace. But at this time, both the government and private kilns there were busy producing cricket jars. The blue-and-white cricket jars made by the government kiln there were in great demand by high officials and the nobles. Even today, a blue-and-white cricket jar made during the Xuande years was highly favored by collectors.

Lady Sun Supersedes the Empress; Empress Hu Is Converted to Buddhism.

In the third month of the 15th year of Yongle (1417), the 18-year-old Zhu Zhanji, the grandson of the emperor and heir apparent, married Lady Hu under his grandfather's arrangement. The marriage was considered a late one in the Ming court. When Zhu Zhanji was 12 years old, his grandfather was already looking for someone for him. Recommended by relatives of the imperial family, a Sun family's

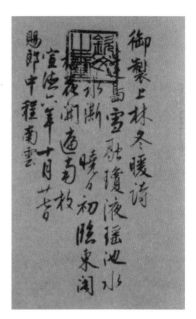

"Warm Winter in the Woods," a poem written by the emperor.

10-year-old daughter was taken to the palace to be brought up by Zhu Zhanji's mother. The two youngsters played together and became an ideal pair. But later, when it was time to confer titles after they were married, Sun was only given the title of an imperial concubine. The reason why was not explained in official history books. Historical novels say that an astronomical official prophesied that a good woman must be found in the Shandong area to be the empress. A woman of the Hu family in Jining was eventually chosen.

Zhu Zhanji liked Sun better because she was clever and more beautiful. But he could not disobey his grandfather's arrangement. Eight years later, after Zhu Zhanji had ascended to the throne, while coffering the title of empress on Hu, he promoted Sun by three grades and made her the honorable imperial concubine, next in rank only to the empress. According to regulations of the Ming court, no gold seal was to be given to the honorable imperial concubine. But Zhu Zhanji insisted that the honorable imperial concubine was to be treated the same as the empress and a gold document and a gold seal were given to each of the two women. He also broke many of the established rules in his later years.

According to history books, Empress Hu was a gentle and quiet woman, but did not give birth to any child. Honorable Imperial Concubine Sun was also childless, but she played a trick and took a pregnant woman to the palace. When the woman gave birth to a baby, she declared that the baby was hers. Even though there were people who knew the secrete, no one dared to speak about it. Following "the age-old tradition that the mother is honored on account of her son," Zhu Zhanji made a big fanfare of it and staged a grand ceremony to confer the title of crown prince on the adopted boy who was only two months and four days old. He also wanted to depose the empress.

Picture of Emperor Xuande hunting on horseback.

Empress Sun, the second empress of Emperor Xuande.

Many of the court officials were against it and said that there was no precedent to depose a faultless empress and that it would mar the emperor's reputation. Several of the court officials were thrown into prison because they were strongly opposed to it. After discussing it with a few confidants, Zhu Zhanji found a way that would not harm his reputation and would depose the empress. The way was to gave the empress a hint that she should voluntarily relinquished her title of empress.

As things were already what they were, the empress tendered her "resignation" for the reason that she "suffered from many ailments and was childless." Zhu Zhanji gladly accepted her resignation and moved her to another palace and conferred the title of empress on Lady Sun in grand style. Empress Hu later was converted to Buddhism and given the title of "Calm and Benevolent Master of the Buddhist Law." She died in 1443 at the age of 43 and was buried at the Golden Hill on the outskirts of the capital with a ceremony for a low-ranking imperial concubine. Only after the death of Empress Sun was her memorial ceremony restored to one for an empress. Her tomb was named "Tomb of the Courteous and Magnanimous Empress," the only solitary tomb of the Ming imperial family.

A panoramic view of Yuling.

Yuling

Built in 1464, Yuling is the tomb of Zhu Qizhen, the sixth emperor of the Ming dynasty, where he was buried together with his Empress Qian and Honorable Imperial Concubine Zhou, mother of the crown prince.

The Child Emperor Is Assisted by Three Teachers; He Is Taken Prisoner by the Mongols at Tumu.

In the early spring of the 10th year of Xuande (1435), Zhu Qizhen, the nine-year-old young emperor was placed in the throne. As he was too young to direct government affairs, he was assisted by court officials of his late father. Among them Yang Shiqi, Yang Rong and Yang Fu were teachers of the late emperor, who enjoyed high prestige in both the government and among the people. Supported by the empress dowager (Zhu Qizhen's grandmother), the three Yangs played an important role in running the government and ensured the smooth operation of the state machine.

One of the things waiting for immediate decision was establishing the capital. In the 18th year of Yongle (1420), after the construction of the imperial palace in Beijing was completed, it was announced during the Spring Festival of the following year that the capital was to be moved from Nanjing to Beijing. But before 100 days after the ceremony, the three main halls of the palace, Fengtian, Huagai and Jinshen, were burned down by a sudden fire and were not reconstructed during the Hongxi and Xuande reigns, because the court hesitated about moving the capital. Supervised by the three Yangs, the reconstruction of the palace was started after the burial ceremony for Zhu Zhanji. In the 10th month of the first year of Zhengtong (1436), the construction of the nine city gates was formally started. The city wall was built on the foundation of the earthen wall of Khanbalig of the Yuan dynasty, moved slightly southward and reinforced with bricks. The three great halls of the palace were rebuilt and the living quarters of the emperor and empress, the Qianqing Hall and Kunning Hall, were completely redecorated. The stone statues along the Divine Path leading to the tomb area at Heavenly Longevity Mountain were also completed at the same time. In the 11th month of the sixth year of Zhengtong (1436), the young emperor Zhu Qizhen was able to announce publicly that Beijing was the capital of the Ming dynasty.

The following year, the grand empress dowager, who supervised the living quarters of the palace, passed away. In the two or three years around this time, the three Yangs, who handled state affairs on behalf of the emperor, also left the world. The authority for handling state affairs was restored to Zhu Qizhen after his marriage. But Zhu Qizhen, who was totally free from worrying about food and clothing, did not seem to be interested in politics. He handed all court affairs to a grand eunuch named Wang Zhen, who was the emperor's rudimentary teacher and only trusted person.

In the summer of the 14th year of Zhengtong (1449), report arrived from north of the Great Wall that Yexian, the chieftain of the Mongol Waci tribe, had invaded Datong with his cavalrymen. Upon hearing the news, Wang Zhen urged the emperor to follow the example of his forefathers and lead an expedition against the invaders. Although Zhu Qizhen had never been away from the capital, he approved his teacher Wang's proposal in spite of the advice of many court officials against it because the army was not ready for a long expedition. The young and willful emperor said that he had made up his mind and ordered the army to leave the capital in two days. A ceremony to pledge resolution was held on the 15th day of the

Main gate of Yuling.

Yuling. Ruins of its Lingen Hall are in the tree shade..

seventh month and the army marched out of the capital the following day.

This expeditionary force was known to be of half a million men. It marched out in total disorder and without sufficient food and fodder. As the units from different places had no unified command, the men were lax in discipline. Before they had marched very far to the other side of the Great Wall, some soldiers died of hunger and thirst. In some unit, half of the soldiers deserted. When Zhu Qizhen reached Datong on the first day of the eighth month, Yexian had already withdrawn. It started to rain heavily for days. A few skirmishes were fought near Datong, but the Ming army was defeated at each one of them. Zhu Qizhen lost all interest in this excursion. He stayed at Datong only for one day and ordered the army to march back on the third day of the eighth month.

Upon hearing the withdrawal of the Ming army, Yexian tailed the Ming army with his cavalry and fought a guerrilla war. The Ming army was forced to fight back along the way. On the 14th day of the eighth month, Zhu Qizhen and his army arrived at a place named Tumubao. Wang Zhen, who did not have even the most basic military common sense, acted on his own and arranged to have the emperor stay at Tumubao, a spot short of water supply, instead of letting the emperor stay in the nearby city of Huailai and the army to camp at a place with a plentiful supply of water and grass. The following day, the 15th day of the eighth month, was the Mid-Autumn Festival. The emperor and his army were at first harassed by Yexian's Mongol cavalry, who came in increasing numbers and encircled the Ming army. At noon the following day, when men of the Ming army, who had not drunk a drop of water for two days and one night, were eager to look for water, the Mongol cavalry started an attack. The men of the Ming army, claimed to be half a million strong, were either killed or fled. Dozens of senior officials died in battle. Wang Zhen was killed by one of his guard officers. Seeing that the situation was hopeless, Zhu Qizhen sat on the ground and shouted in a loud voice, "I am the emperor! I am the emperor!" Instead of hurting him, the Mongol cavalrymen put him on a horse and took him with them as a hostage.

The emperor of the Great Ming Empire thus became a prisoner of the Mongols. In history, this incident was known as the "Tumu Incident."

Zhu Qizhen Is Honored in the Desert Area; The Father Emperor Becomes a Prisoner in South Palace.

Escorted by Mongol cavalry, Zhu Qizhen was taken from place to place and eventually to the camp of

Yexian. The latter never thought he would meet the emperor on such an occasion. He hurriedly invited the emperor into the tent and treated him with respect. This was because Yexian and his followers had been to Beijing several times to deliver tribute of horses to the Ming court. He had performed obeisance to Zhu Qizhen and received rewards from the emperor on several occasions. As soon as he saw the emperor, he knew who he was.

It was said that Yexian's mother was a woman from Suzhou in South China. Influenced by the Han culture since childhood, Yexian admired ardently the culture of the Central Plains. His attack on Datong was actually caused by his anger for Wang Zhen, who worked hand in glove with local officials to embezzle the silver awarded to him by the Ming court. The sudden arrival of the emperor pleased him very much. It was really a case of "Good fortune lies within bad." Zhu Qizhen thus became an honored guest on the grassland. But he could only sleep in a tent, drink milk tea and go out in a two-wheeled wooden ox-cart.

During the year that followed, Zhu Qizhen on the grassland had sent men to Beijing several times to ask for clothes, silver and gifts for Yexian to express his gratitude. Yexian had also led his cavalry and Zhu Qizhen to Datong, Xuanfu and Beijing to give back the emperor to the Ming court. But by court order, the city gates in all the places were closed to them. The Ming court refused to take the emperor back. This happened because after the capture of Zhu Qizhen by the Mongols, a younger brother named Zhu Qiyu, born of a different mother, was made the new emperor. Yexian's repeated requests to send Zhu Qizhen back presented a problem for the Ming court.

In the eighth month, the following year (1450),

when Beijing again sent men to the grassland to deliver gifts, Yexian insisted on sending Zhu Qizhen back to Beijing and held a farewell banquet for the occasion. The new emperor in Beijing had no choice but to send two officials to the Juyong Pass to take Zhu Qizhen back in a horse-drawn carriage. Outside the palace's Eastern Flowery Gate, the two brothers greeted each other in a few words, and Zhu Qizhen was taken to the South Palace.

The South Palace formed a detached courtyard outside the imperial palace. After Zhu Qizhen moved into it, the tightly closed gate was watched by guards. Things were regularly delivered to it, but no officials had been seen to have gone into or come out of it. To prevent outsiders to intrude into it, all the trees around the walls were cut down. Zhu Qizhen, the so-called father emperor, thus became a closely watched prisoner. It was said that Zhu Qizhen lived in straitened circumstances. Empress Qian who lived with him had to sell all her jewels and do some needle work to earn some money.

The seven years of life in the South Palace were a very painful experience for Zhu Qizhen, emperor of the Zhengtong reign.

The Emperor Is Enthroned Again; Thousands of People Are Promoted.

Zhen Qizhen lived in the South Palace for seven years. Although he was the father emperor in name, his circumstances were reduced beyond his imagination. What was further beyond his imagination was that good fortune would befall on him again one day. The day arrived as a result of help given to him by some officials who served at the time when he was in the throne. It was really a case of the two lines of a poem: "Among the sons and brothers east of the river are many talents; who knows they may one day stage a comeback?"

The precarious opportunity presented itself on the 28th day of the 12th month in the seventh year of Jingtai (1456). It was the lunar New Year's Eve, or Spring Festival. A jubilant atmosphere prevailed both inside and outside the palace. The young emperor was suddenly pulled down by illness at this time. Some court officials began to whisper to one another about who was to succeed to the throne if the emperor could not recover. Since the young emperor's son had died young, the only candidate was Zhu Qianshen, the eldest son of the emperor's elder brother, Zhu Qizhen. Next came Zhu Qizhen, the father emperor, himself. These whispers were wild guesses made by court officials in private. As the saying goes: "A casual word may reveal much to an attentive listener." The words were overheard by Shi Heng, commander-in-chief of the five garrison battalions in Beijing, a frontier general of both courage and resourcefulness, who had been promoted when Zhu Qizhen was in the throne. When he saw that the opportunity for action had arrived, Shi Heng called together his confidants and started to plot. They concluded that it was better to act immediately than waiting for the death of Emperor Jingtai before the father emperor was to succeed to the throne and that they could gain both fame and benefits if they acted immediately.

According to age-old customs, there was a fortnight of holiday for government offices during the Spring Festival. In the still of the night on the 16th day of the first month in the eighth year of Jingtai (1457), Shi Heng and others assembled a group of able army officers and headed straight for the South Palace, where they crashed through the gate, broke the wall and put a yellow robe on Zhu Qizhen and took him away in a small sedan-chair. The father emperor did not know what was happening and thought it was the end of his life. He felt relieved only when Shi Heng told him the purpose of their action. When they reached the Eastern Flowery Gate, the gate was tightly closed. According to regulations, there were eunuchs on duty inside. Only urgent written messages were allowed to be delivered through the crack in the gate, but no one was allowed to open the gate. In the face of this situation, the only way out was for the father emperor to present himself. After Zhu Qizhen had shouted several times, "I am the father emperor," the eunuchs inside opened the gate. The group walked directly to the Fengtian Hall. When Zhu Qizhen sat down on the throne, it was already daylight. Bells and drums began to ring and boom in the palace. It was the 17th day of the first month and time to hold the first morning court after the New

The Inner Red Gate as seen from an elevation.

Year holidays. When the civil and military officials took up their positions, they found that the emperor had changed into another person. This is known in history as the "Gate Crashing Incident."

After sitting again in the throne, Zhu Qizhen dispensed rewards to people according to their contributions. Shi Heng was made the Duke of Loyalty. At Shi Heng's recommendation, the first group of senior and junior officials to be promoted totaled 3,180 men. Zhu Qizhen wrote clearly in the official document: "Those who crashed the gate are to be promoted three grades and those who guarded the gate to protect the emperor were to be promoted one grade." Tens of thousands profited as a result of the incident.

The ailing Zhu Qiyu was deposed on the first day of the second month, given the title of Prince of Cheng and moved to the West Palace, where he died about 10 days later. He was buried as a prince at the foot of the Golden Hill in western Beijing. The tomb was also known as the Jingtai Tomb.

Zhu Qizhen Shows Kindness in His Last Words; Imperial Concubine Zhou Fights for Place in the Tomb.

After his restoration, Zhu Qizhen changed the name of his reign to Tianshun, meaning that his restoration was "following the will of Heaven". It was soon the eighth year of Tianshun (1464), when people in the whole country warmly celebrated the Spring Festival at the beginning of the new year. On New Year's Day, when the emperor received the civil and mili-

A portrait of Emperor Zhengtong in the sitting position.

tary officials and foreign envoys who had come to congratulate, he probably had drunk too much at the banquet. On the following day, eunuchs reported that the emperor was not quite well and needed some rest. As all the government offices were closed for the holidays and people were taking a rest in the winter, no one paid any attention to it. When the court officials returned to work on the 16th day of the first month, they were handed a document that recorded by a eunuch what the emperor had said and requested them to polish and revise the wording and distribute it. After reading the document, the court officials could not make head or tail of it. They stayed in the office for a whole day and night and were unable to give any suggestions for its revision. In the early morning the following day (17th of the first month), a report arrived from the palace that the emperor had passed away in the Qianqing Hall. (It was the same day seven years ago when Zhu Qizhen was restored.) The unrevised document thus became Zhu Qizhen's last words.

In addition to dealing with such state affairs as reducing taxes and extending relief to victims of natural disasters, the last words also contained instructions for the emperor's family affairs:

1. The sons and daughters of Emperor Jianwen who had been imprisoned during the Yongle reign should be released and allowed to marry freely.

2. Abolishing the custom of burying imperial concubines and court women with the dead emperor.

3. Restoring the title on Empress Hu who had been converted to Buddhism during the Xuande reign, and

holding sacrificial ceremonies in memory of her as an empress.

4. Empress Qian's position had already been established. She should be served filially for the rest of her life and buried with me when she died.

What happened later showed that Zhu Qizhen's worries about burying her with him was not unnecessary. Four years later, when the 42-year-old Empress Qian died in the sixth month of the fourth year of Chenghua, her burial with the emperor in Yuling as instructed by the emperor was strongly opposed by Imperial Concubine Zhou, the emperor's own mother. While court officials argued on the ground of the late emperor's instructions, the reigning emperor, Zhu Jianshen, was placed in an awkward predicament. To show their determination to follow the ancestral traditions and the late emperor's instructions, more than 40 of the senior court officials knelt outside the palace gate from nine in the morning to five in the afternoon, requesting Imperial Concubine Zhou to agree to burying Empress Qian with the emperor. Many of them actually fainted in the hot noon sun. At sunset, Imperial Concubine Zhou was forced to agree to the burial together. It was said that the court officials were wild with joy to show their loyalty to the late emperor.

Imperial Concubine Zhou's assent, however, was conditional. Empress Qian's coffin was not to be place side by side with the coffin of the emperor. The place was to be reserved for herself when she died. The court officials had no choice but to do their next best, which was to place Empress Qian's coffin in the left side-chamber in the tomb and had the passage to the main chamber blocked up.

Jingtailing

Jingtailing, also known as Jing Emperor's Tomb, at the foot of the Golden Hill in the western outskirts of Beijing, is the tomb where Zhu Qiyu, the seventh emperor of the Ming dynasty, and Empress Wang were buried together. It was built in 1457 in the style of a prince's tomb. When the title of emperor was restored to Zhu Qiyu, the surface structures were rebuilt in the style of an emperor's tomb. It is the only emperor's tomb not built in the Heavenly Longevity Mountain tomb area.

Absence of the Emperor Disgraces the Court; Zhu Qiyu Takes the Throne in the Crisis.

On the 16th day of the eighth month in the 14th year of the Zhengtong reign (1449), the all-powerful Emperor Zhu Qizhen of the Great Ming dynasty was captured by Mongol cavalry at Tumubao. When the bad news about the destruction of the entire Ming army of hundreds of thousands of men reached Beijing the following day, the court and the whole capital were

The stele pavilion at Jingtailing.

thrown into a great confusion. Beating their chests and stamping their feet, the civil and military officials in the capital did not know what to do. There were all kinds of talks in the capital. Some suggested that the capital should be moved back to Nanjing immediately. At this critical moment, Yu Qian, the Vice-President of the Board of War, made a cool analysis of the situation and put forward some suggestions to the empress dowager (Emperor Xuande's Empress Sun and natural mother of Zhu Qizhen) to pacify the mood of the people and maintain control of the situation. His suggestions were: 1. Since it is important that "a country should not be without a ruler for a single day," the position of Zhu Qiyu as the regent should be strengthened to ensure the smooth running of the government. 2. Army units stationed in the various places in the country should be assembled in Beijing to readjust the defense of the capital and the frontiers. For fear that new problems might crop up, the empress dowager added that Zhu Qizhen's two-year-old son, Zhu Jianshen, should be made the crown prince to ensure the legitimacy and temporary nature of his uncle Zhu Qiyu's regency. The empress dowager, however, did not expect that the regency of Zhu Qiyu would cause a zigzag in the history of the Ming dynasty.

Zhu Qiyu was only a few months younger than Zhu Qizhen, his elder brother born of a different mother. He was conferred the title of Prince of Cheng, but had not been given a fief. His natural mother, Lady Wu, was originally a maid in the house of Zhu Gaoxi, the Prince of Han. When Zhu Zhanji, the emperor, led an army to suppress the rebellion of the Prince of Han, he saw the clever and beautiful Wu and took her back to Beijing. For fear that people might gossip behind him because Wu came from his uncle's house, he put Wu in a house outside the palace. Two years later, Wu gave birth to Zhu Qiyu, Zhu Zhanji's second son, but continued to live outside the palace. It was only when Zhu Zhanji was critically ill that mother and son were taken to the palace.

After the Tumu Incident, Zhu Qiyu, acting as the regent and assisted by Yu Qian and others, reorganized the army and frontier defense. As more than 50 officials of the boards and departments were killed during the Tumu Incident, new and competent officials were appointed to fill the posts. Some of the die-hard followers of Wang Zhen were also dealt with. The political situation was soon stabilized. In this aspect, Zhu Qiyu had made his share of contributions when he acted as the regent during the national crisis.

A New Emperor Sits in the Throne; Empress Wang Suffers for Her Outspokenness.

Without the Tumu Incident, Zhu Qiyu would never have dreamt that he would one day sit in the throne. When Yu Qian and others urged him to punish Wang Zhen's followers, he hesitated because he was afraid that he himself might be involved in it. One day while holding court, the officials became so agitated that they started to attack three followers of Wang Zhen physically on the spot and beat them to death. Zhu Qiyu became scared and wanted to run away, but Yu Qian pulled him back. He had no choice but to say that "the crafty ones should be eliminated and their properties confiscated to vent the people's anger."

Only then did the court officials cheered and left. This happened on the ninth day after the capture of Zhu Qizhen. In the days that followed, the civil and military officials reported everything to Zhu Qiyu. Even though many of the ideas for dealing with problems were not his, he became quite smug as he began to enjoy the immense power in his hands. Since no one knew when his brother, the emperor, would return, he hinted to the court officials that they should try to convince the empress dowager that he should be made the new emperor. Taking his hint readily, the court officials did their best to convince the empress dowager until she consented. Zhu Qiyu was thus enthroned on the sixth day of the ninth month as the new emperor. He was addressed as "Your Majesty" instead of "Your Highness," and the title of reign changed to Jingtai.

As time went by, Zhu Qiyu began to feel uncomfortable about having Zhu Qizhen's son, Zhu Jianshen, as the legitimate successor to the throne and started to think about replacing the crown prince with his own son. But the court officials maintained that the replacing should not be carried out immediately because Zhu Qiyu's son was not yet two years old and not born of his first wife. Empress Wang was also strongly against it and said that it was already not proper to lock up the emperor's brother in the South Palace and that since the crown prince had committed no wrongs, it was not right the depose him. Zhu Qiyu was not pleased at all with the court officials and Empress Wang, but he had no place to vent his anger. It was at this moment, a toady government official in the far Guangxi frontier heard about the struggle over the crown prince and saw that his chance of promotion had come. He wrote a memorial to the throne requesting the replacement of the crown prince. Zhu Qiyu showed the memorial to the court officials and asked them to sign their names on it to show wither they were for or against it. Under tremendous pressure, the officials had no alternative but to agree. In the fifth month of the fourth year of the Jingtai reign, Zhu Qiyu eventually succeeded in installing his own son who was not yet four years old as the crown prince and demote his nephew Zhu Qianshen and made him the Prince of Yi. Empress Wang, who was against replacing the crown prince, was also deposed and the new crown prince's natural mother, Hang, became the empress. The struggle over the replacement of the crown prince thus came to an end. But Heaven did not always follow man's will. The new crown prince died of illness in the 11th month of that year and Zhu Qiyu was left without a successor.

After her deposition, Empress Wang was moved to another palace, where she lived a quiet and leisurely life with her two daughters. When Zhu Jianshen became emperor, he did not forget his aunt's virtue and courageous fight on just grounds for his rights and treated her kindly. When she died in the 12th month of the first year of Zhengde (1506) at the age of 62, she was buried together with the emperor in the Jingtai tomb as suggested by court officials.

Maoling

Maoling, built in 1487, is the tomb of Zhu Jianshen, the eighth emperor of the Ming dynasty. Buried with him here are his second empress, Wang, and two imperial concubines, Ji and Shao.

Remains of the foundation of the main hall at Maoling.

The Crown Prince Is Slighted and Deposed; The Emperor Learns Social Morals from Operas.

When Zhu Qiyu was running the court after the Tumu Incident, the two-year-old Zhu Jianshen was the crown prince. But in the power struggle to rename the crown prince during the Jingtai reign, he was deposed when he was seven years old and became the Prince of Yi. After his father was restored to the throne in the first year of Tianshun (1457), he became the crown prince again. His tumultuous experience reflected the fierce struggle in the palace. When his father died eight years later, he succeeded to the throne at 18 and became known as Emperor Chenghua in history.

Historians generally take the ascendance of Zhu Jianshen to the throne as the beginning of the middle period of the Ming dynasty, a period characterized by increasing corruption of the rulers. Officials were appointed simply by a piece of paper handed out from the palace by a eunuch known as the "appointment relaying officer." The civil examinations system existed in name only. Secondly, land ownership became increasingly concentrated. The bureaucrat-landlords desperately enlarged their land and properties. Even the emperor and empress had their private land, known as "imperial estates." As members of the imperial family and clan followed suit, the peasants were burdened by heavy taxation. As people became destitute and homeless, peasants rose frequently in revolt.

As bad news trickled continually into the palace, Zhu Jianshen gradually lost confidence in his officials and relied increasingly on the eunuchs near him. As a result, power began to be concentrated in the hands of the eunuchs. The most villainous one of the eunuchs was Wang Zhi. As head of the Eastern Yard, a spy organization, he reported directly to the emperor. Even the other spy organizations, such as the Silk Uniformed Guards and the Western Yard, were under his surveillance. He had the power to arrest, imprison and kill people inside and outside the capital. Under his despotic oppression, both the officials and the common people lived under his menace.

Zhu Jianshen never came out of the palace. Besides playing around with his concubines, he favored the plays and operas composed and staged by eunuchs, because they were not only diversions from boredom, but also helped him to understand social

The Inner Red Gate of Maoling.

trends. The following passages from plays had produced certain influence on the emperor:

1. A young eunuch, named Ah Chou, played the part of a drunkard, who flung abuses in the street and acted wildly. As he was watched by a large crowd, someone warned him, saying that a certain government official was coming. The drunkard continued to utter abuses. Someone else then said to him that the emperor was here. But the drunkard went on with his abusive acts. When someone said that Eunuch Wang was here, the drunkard immediately stood at attention with the utmost deference. When people asked the young eunuch why he was not afraid of the emperor, but Eunuch Wang. The drunkard said that he only knew there was Eunuch Wang but not the emperor. From then on, Zhu Jianshen gradually began to keep a watchful eye on Wang Zhi.

2. During the reign of Zhu Jianshen, official posts were openly bought and sold and bribery was widespread. People of knowledge and vision were pushed aside. In view of this situation, the eunuchs staged a play with a senior court official in it, who was out to appoint people to official posts. When the first man was brought in, he asked him what was his name. The man said that his name was Public Opinion. The senior official said, "Public Opinion had no use today. Out with you." The second man came in and said that his name was Justice. The senior official said, "Justice does not work nowadays." When the third man came in and said that his name was Muddle-headed. The senior official smiled and nodded his head, saying, "The muddle-headed ones are useful today," and appointed him to an important post. The play added a footnote to officialdom of the Chenghua reign. It was said that the system of "appointment

A blank stone stele.

relaying officer" was abolished after the emperor had seen the play.

3. During the Chenghua reign, officials of all levels rode rough shod over the ordinary people. They occupied people's land and drafted laborers to build their own houses and even dispatched soldiers for private work. Without proper training, the Ming army was defeated several times by the intruding Mongol tribes. In one of the plays watched by Zhu Jianshen, a man played the role of Xiang Yu, the Conqueror of the state of Chu, of 2,000 years ago. He declared on the stage, "I am taking 6,000 of my army of sons of the people to fight a life-and-death battle against Liu Bang, my rival." Someone then corrected him, saying, "Wrong. Xiang Yu led an army of 8,000 sons of the people. Why have you reduced the number?" Xiang Yu answered with shame, "I can't help it. 2,000 of my men were drafted to build houses for an official." How

Zhu Jianshen felt when he watched the play is not known. The corruption of officialdom at the time was truthfully reflected in this play.

Imperial Concubine Wan Is Doted on as Never Before; Zhu Jianshen Deposes the Empress on a Flimsy Excuse.

Imperial Concubine Wan was named Zhen'er when she was young. Born in the fifth year of Xuande (1430), she was taken to the palace when she was only four years old. When she was older, she began to serve Imperial Concubine Sun (Zhu Jianshen's grandmother) as a waiting maid. As she was both clever and agreeable, she was much favored by Sun. After the Tumu Incident, Sun sent this 19-year-old girl to look after her two-year-old son Zhu Jianshen, the crown prince. It was under the protective wings of Wu that Zhu Jianshen spent his childhood and youthful days. This special environment and relationship produced in Zhu Jianshen a psychological reliance on Wu as an elder sister and mother. As Zhu Jianshen grew older, he found himself in love with the woman who was 17 years older than himself.

In the eighth year of Tianshun (1464), a chance presented itself to give a name to their close relationship. In the first month of that year, the 17-year-old Zhu Jianshen succeeded to the throne. According to traditional customs, the next item on the agenda was to arrange the marriage of the young emperor. Zhu Jianshen insisted on making the 35-year-old Wan the empress. As his mother, the empress dowager, was firmly against it, it resulted in a sharp conflict between mother and son. The conflict lasted for a period of time before a compromise was reached. On the 21st day of the seventh month of that year, a Lady Wu, who was a year younger than the emperor, was made the empress, and Wan was given the title of imperial concubine. The empress dowager asked her son afterwards, "Wan is not beautiful. Why do you like her?" Zhu Jianshen said frankly, "I could not go to sleep without Wan's caressing. It has nothing to do with whether she is beautiful or not." After listening to him, the empress dowager had no choice but to give way to him.

No one had ever expected that on the morning of the 22nd day of the eighth month, immediately after the young emperor's honeymoon, a decree was issued deposing Empress Wu and moving her to another palace. The decree said in brief that Empress Wu be-

Gate to the grave of Honorable Imperial Concubine Wan.

haved badly in language and action and rudely violated proprieties. History books wrote that Empress Wu was a woman of excellent character. After marriage, Imperial Concubine Wan repeatedly provoked the empress because she thought she was favored by the emperor. Angered by her provocations, the empress hit Wan. Wan wailed and wept in front of Zhu Jianshen, so the young emperor issued a decree deposing the empress to vent Wan's spleen. Zhu Jianshen intended to make Wan the empress, but the empress dowager intervened. In the middle of the 10th month, a Lady Wang who had long been in the palace was made the empress. Wan was still the second wife of the emperor in rank. Since Empress Wang was a virtuous woman, who did not fight for the emperor's affections, the rear quarters of the palace became somewhat more peaceful.

It was soon the second month of the second year of Chenghua. The 36-year-old Imperial Concubine Wan gave birth to a son. Zhu Jianshen was highly pleased by the birth of his first son. Besides celebrations in the palace, officials were sent to famous towns and the Five Sacred Mountains to pray to Heaven for the protection of his son. When the son was a month old, Wan was conferred the title of Honorable Imperial Concubine. But it was to be regretted that the son died of illness in the 11th month of that year before he was a year old. It was a blow to Zhu Jianshen, but he continued to favor Wan.

During the Spring Festival in the 23rd year of Chenghua (1487), Wan was angered by a palace maid. When she angrily scolded her, she was choked to death when she was 58 years old. Zhu Jianshen was overcome with sorrow. He said in tears that because Wan had died, he could not live any longer. Sure enough, he also passed away eight months later, following immediately behind Wan when he was only 41 years old.

Ji Shu Hides Herself Outside the Palace; The Son Sees His Father for the First Time at Six.

Ji, the daughter of a local tribal chief of the Miao people in Guangxi, was summoned to the palace when she was a young girl. As she was intelligent, careful in doing things and knew how to read and write, she was made a literary maid to look after the palace's treasure house when she grew up. Zhu Jianshen met her by accident one day. As she answered all his questions correctly and clearly, the emperor was pleased with her and took her to his bedroom. Ji became pregnant before long.

In those days, Imperial Concubine Wan was the

woman most favored by the emperor. After the early death of her son, in particular, she was jealous of any woman in the rear quarters of the palace who had become pregnant. A son was born to Lady Bai, the Concubine of Virtue, and was made the crown prince. Wan played a trick and had the son poisoned to death. Any other women who had become pregnant was forced to abort. When Ji was pregnant, she moved to the

Picture of Blessing and Longevity painted by Emperor Chenghua.

Training Birds, a picture showing Emperor Chenghua playing with eunuchs.

Hall of Peace and Happiness outside the palace on the excuse that she had a tumor in her stomach. The Hall of Peace and Happiness was in an out-of-the-way place, where palace maids lived in old age. Ji gave birth to a boy there without many people knowing about it.

In the 11th year of Chenghua (1475), while Zhang Min, a eunuch, was combing the emperor's hair in front of a mirror, Zhu Jianshen said to himself with a sigh that he was growing old and still did not have a son to succeed him. Seeing the emperor was very sad, Zhang Min quickly kneeled down and reported to him that the son borne by Ji was already six years old. Zhu Jianshen was delighted and immediately went to see him. He moved Ji to a place known as the Hall of Eternal Life and asked the empress dowager to look after his son. The six-year-old boy was given a formal name — Zhu Youtang.

This happened in the middle of the fifth month. On the 28th day of the sixth month, news of the death of the natural mother of the emperor's son came out of the palace and aroused all kinds of comments. It was said that Ji was poisoned by arsenic placed in her food by Wan. After her death, Ji was conferred the title of Fair Concubine and buried at the foot of the Golden Hill in western Beijing. When her son Zhu Youtang succeeded to throne 12 years later, he moved the remains of his mother to Maoling as an empress.

Tailing

Built in 1505, Tailing is the tomb of Zhu Youtang, the ninth emperor of the Ming dynasty, where he was buried together with his Empress Zhang.

Front gate of Tailing.

The Young Emperor Is on Guard Against Palace Plot; Imposters of the Emperor's Relatives Are Shown Up.

In the fifth month of the 11th year of Chenghua (1475), the six-year-old Zhu Youtang was taken to the palace from the Hall of Peace and Happiness. When his mother died an unnatural death a month later, he was placed under the guardianship of his grandmother, the empress dowager. After he became the crown prince half a year later, grandmother and grandson still lived together. The grandmother was with him all the time and looked after him in every aspect of his life to prevent any untoward thing from happening to him. On a festival day, Imperial Concubine Wan invited him to her palace to show her concern for him. Before he left, his grandmother warned him repeatedly about what to do and what not to do and sent some competent palace maids to go with him. When he was asked to eat in Wan's Virtue-manifesting Palace, he said he was not hungry. When he was given water to drink, he said there might be poison in the water. Imperial Concubine Wan was so angered by him, she took to her bed by illness for days.

The 17-year-old Zhu Youtang succeeded to the throne in the ninth month of the 23rd year of Chenghua (1487), changed the title of reign to Hongzhi and started "to govern on behalf of Heaven" as the emperor.

Out of gratitude for and in memory of his mother, Zhu Youtang sent eunuchs to Guangxi to look for members and relatives of the Ji family after he had ascended to the throne. An old eunuch remembered that because Lady Ji was still young when she was taken to the palace, she could only remember that her family was in Guangxi's Hexian County. This made the search for Lady Ji's family a most difficult one. Assisted by local governments, the eunuchs eventually found two Ji brothers in a remote mountain village and took them to Beijing as members of Lady Ji's family. Zhu Youtang treated them most kindly by giving them houses and servants and assigning them to official posts. He also had the graves of the Ji family rebuilt. But before the emperor had done all the good things for them, a eunuch named Lu Kai suddenly came forward and said that Lady Ji's original family name was not Ji, but Li, and her home not in Hexian, but in Lianshan. Zhu Youtang was utterly puzzled.

Surface tower.

A screen wall in front of the tomb.

Some officials then suggested that they must find the
true one even if they were deceived many times. Officials were sent out to investigate repeatedly, but none
of the local officials could tell the whereabouts of the
Li family. Some officials from the Board of Personnel
and Board of Rites, known for their careful performance of duty, were sent to investigate by disguising
themselves as ordinary people. The whole truth eventually came out. The eunuch Lu Kai was from Guangxi.
When Zhu Youtang was the crown prince, he sent
members of his family secretly to look for members
of Lady Ji's family. When he learned that all the members of the Ji family were killed in battles against the
Ming army, he asked his uncle to impose himself as a
member of Lady Ji's family and receive land allotted
to him. Even the village's name was changed to Kind-

ness-receiving Village. When the imposters were exposed, they were all punished by exile to the frontier areas. The local officials who failed to perform their duties properly were also punished.

Later, when "no traces of the past could be found," Zhu Youtang adopted the proposal of the Board of Rites and had an ancestral temple built outside the west gate of Guilin in Guangxi with ancestral tablets in it for holding memorial ceremonies. It ended his eager but fruitless search of his ancestors.

The Emperor Worships Buddha and Makes Pills of Immortality; He is Hoodwinked by Eunuchs Who Take Away His Money.

Zhu Youtang lived deep in the palace and rarely came out. Besides offering sacrifices to Heaven at the Temple of Heaven in the southern part of Beijing, he had never been away from the capital. Misled by the eunuch Li Guang, he devoted most his energy to worshipping Buddha and holding Buddhist rituals. He then went on to make pills of immortality in the hope of living for ever. He expressed himself in two lines of a poem: "Staying in quietude and cultivating the vital energy to nourish myself, I can become my true self when I am in perfect health."

To pray for the emperor's good fortune, the eunuch Li Guang proposed that an imposing pavilion, named Beauty-nurturing Pavilion, was to be built on top of the Longevity Hill north of the palace. Soon after the pavilion was completed, the emperor's eldest young daughter died and a fire broke out in the

Pure and Quiet Palace where the emperor's grandmother lived. The grandmother censured him, saying that if the emperor went on to rely on Li Guang for everything, the whole family would be destroyed. For fear of being punished, Li Guang committed suicide. Zhu Youtang believed that Li Guang had become an immortal and gone to Heaven. He sent men to Li's luxurious house to search for secret formulas for becoming an immortal. The men found some books, which recorded amounts of white rice or yellow rice delivered to him. The books actually recorded the bribes given to Li Guang by government officials. The white rice referred to silver, and yellow rice, to gold. Since so many of the officials were involved, the bribery was overlooked because of the Chinese saying, "The law provides no punishment for the multitude." But Zhu Youtang still refused to come to his senses and continued to swallow pills to seek longevity until the poisonous elements in the pills made him feel hot and dry all over. On the seventh day of the fifth month in the 18th year of Hongzhi, he died while his mouth and nose continued to bleed at the age of 36.

Stove for burning elegiac address written on silk at Tailing.

Kangling

Kangling is the burial place of Zhu Houzhao (1491-1521), the 10th emperor of the Ming dynasty, and his Empress Zhang (1493-1535).

Entrance to Kangling.

The New Emperor Visits Brothels in Disguise; The Leopard House Is Built for Sensual Pleasure.

Zhu Houzhao, known as Emperor Zhengde, was an intelligent boy when he was young. His formal education started when he was eight. It was said that he had an unusually good memory. He could recite on the following day everything the teacher taught him the previous day, for which he had won the approval of several teachers. Born an active boy, he liked to ride on horseback, shoot arrows and seek all kinds of pleasure. Abetted by eunuchs, he was already a playboy and an expert in training dogs and eagles and keeping horses and fighting cocks before he mounted the throne. His father dotted on him and allowed him to do whatever he like to do. It was only until shortly before his death that his father entrusted him to several of the court officials, saying, "The crown prince is young and fond of pleasure. You must teach him to read books and cultivate his virtue."

When Zhu Houzhao was the crown prince, eight eunuchs headed by Liu Jin were very close to him. As

Surface building in spring.

they and the crown prince were of about the same age, they were interested in the same things and ate, drank and played together. The eight eunuchs were known as the Eight Tigers. After Zhu Houzhao succeeded to the throne at 15, these eunuchs were still his confidants. They played football and the game of throwing arrows into a vase in the rear part of the palace during the day and slipped out of the palace in ordinary clothes at night to find pleasure in restaurants, theaters and brothels.

Zhu Houzhao sought pleasure in many different ways. In 1507, he had a hall built in a side courtyard inside the Western Flowery Gate of the palace with secret rooms in the two wings of the hall, known as the Leopard House, where he kept many rare birds and animals, musicians and maids for his sensual pleasure day and night.

The Emperor Womanizes Noisily at Xuanfu and Fights a Mock Battle Like Children at Play.

As he grew older, Zhu Houzhao began to lose interest in the Leopard House. A eunuch named Jiang Bin who had been with the emperor every day found a opportunity to distinguish himself. Without announcing it, he had a big courtyard with houses around it built in his home town Xuanfu and then recruited a number of musicians and women from honest families to work in it and named the place Country-stabilizing Mansion. When everything was ready, he began to tell the emperor about Xuanfu and

Stone columns of the Flaming Arch.

said, "There are many beautiful women among the musicians in Xuanfu." It was exactly what the emperor liked to hear. After careful planning, the emperor and three of his confidants went out the capital's Victory Gate and started to head for Changping on horseback on a moonlight night in the eight month of the 12th year of Zhengde (1517). The officials on duty at the gate were alarmed and sent men to stop the emperor. When they caught up with the emperor at Changping about 40 kilometers from Beijing, the emperor refused to go back and rode on until he reached the Juyong

Pass of the Great Wall. Imperial Censor Zhang Qin happened to be there making his tour of inspections. On the excuse that the emperor carried no pass, he refused to open the gate. Knowing that he was acting against the ancestral instructions to leave the capital in private and urged by the officials, Zhu Houzhao had no choice but to return to his Leopard House. But his determination to go out of Beijing in disguise had not changed. Several day later, when nobody was watching him, he and several eunuchs disguised themselves as businessmen and slipped out of Beijing in the dark of the night. In view of what had happened last time, he did not go along the main road but followed the country paths to the northwest and stopped at a small village named Yangfang not far from the Juyong Pass. From there, he sent men to reconnoiter. His chance came two days later because Imperial Censor Zhang had left to inspect Baiyangkou. Zhu Houzhao and his followers went out of the pass at night and headed for Xuanfu immediately. A eunuch named Gu Dayong, one of the Eight Tigers, stayed at the Juyong Pass to stop all officials from going out of the pass.

In three years time, Zhu Houzhao visited Xuanfu three times, staying there for more than half a year each time. He even called Xuanfu his "home." History books say that Zhu Houzhao was in high spirits and totally immersed himself in pleasure. There were noisy musical performances in the Country-stabilizing Mansion every night. The emperor often took several people with him and wandered in the streets. When he saw a big house belonging to a well-to-do family, he would knock on the door and enter. The host had to offer him food and drink. If he saw a comely woman there, he would take her to the mansion. Xuanfu was greatly disturbed and thrown into dire confusion.

There was a wine shop in Xuanfu run by a brother and sister. The sister was called Sister Pheonix. When Zhu Houzhao met her by chance and took a fancy to her, he took her to his quarters and became inseparable from her. The brother was given an official post. When Zhu Houzhao was returning to Beijing, he took her with him in a carriage. When they reached the Juyong Pass, Sister Pheonix was struck down by an acute disease and died a sudden death. Overcome with sorrow, Zhu Houzhao had her buried on a mountain slope and ordered the local people to offer sacrifices to her every year. The grave became known as the White Pheonix Grave. The Beijing opera *Wandering Dragon Flirting with the Pheonix* was based on Zhu Houzhao's adventure in Xuanfu.

During his first visit to Xuanfu, Zhu Houzhao staged a farce by creating a frontier skirmish. He conferred the title of "Courageous General and Com-

Imperial path.

mander-in-Chief of All Military Forces" on himself and ordered the military commander of the army in Datong to launch an attack on the Mongol army at the frontier and he would come to his aid with his army units. This skirmish at the frontier resulted in 16 Mongol soldiers killed, while the casualties of the Ming army were 52 killed and 563 seriously wounded. Back in Xuanfu, Zhu Houzhao shamelessly held a victory celebration. It was absolutely ridiculous.

The Emperor Tours Mountains and Rivers with Pleasure; The Boat with the Disguised Fisherman in It Capsizes.

In the sixth month of 1519, a revolt led by Zhen Hao, the Prince of Ning, broke out in Nanchang, Jiangxi. Sending an army to quell the revolt was to Zhu Houzhao a good opportunity to tour the south of the Yangtze River. He personally led an army out of the capital in the eighth month. But the revolt was quickly suppressed by the local government. Zhen Hao and the others were all captured. When Zhu Houzhao received the report of victory in Zhuozhou, his expeditionary army became an army for receiving prisoners. As he traveled on to the south with a light heart, he thoroughly enjoyed the natural scenery along the way.

When he arrived in Nanjing on the 26th day of the 12th month, the beautiful southern scenery enchanted him. The singers and dancers on the Qinhuai River captivated him. He started to settle down there, unwilling to go back to Beijing and forgetting his home and duty.

Zhu Houzhao was a believer in Buddhism. Wherever he went, when he saw a Buddhist temple, he would not only go in to worship and burn incense, but also donate embroidered pennants and flags and Buddhist scriptures. Many of the Buddhist establishments in the south were benefited during Zhu Houzhao's tour of the south.

Time passed quickly. The emperor had stayed in Nanjing for a whole year. Urged by some officials to take the prisoners to the capital, Zhu Houzhao decided to go back to Beijing on the 12th day of the leap eighth month in the 15th year of Zhengde (1520). On the way back to Beijing, he took every opportunity to enjoy himself. He fished at the mouth of the Longjiang River, toured Guazhou in the rain, stayed for the night on the River View Tower and climbed the Golden Mountain in Jijiang, never feeling tired at all.

On the 15th day of the ninth month, the emperor and his entourage arrived at Qingjiang County, where he stayed in the house of Zhang Yang, a eunuch, for three days. When he saw some local fishermen catching fish with a fish spear, he became very curious. Putting on a rain cape and hat, he masqueraded as a fisherman and rowed a boat to the middle of a lake alone to catch fish. The boat capsized. He was saved from drowning when others swam desperately to the middle of the lake. A history book says, "From then on, he did not feel quite himself." It means that after falling into the lake, the emperor became ill.

Zhu Houzhao and his followers returned to Beijing at the end of the year. To celebrate his southern tour and victory in quelling the revolt, a grand ceremony was held in front of the the Zhengyang Gate. The several thousand prisoners and their family members were tied up along the street while the soldiers and civilians were organized to cheer. Zhu Houzhao was dressed in military attire, rode on a horse, carried a sword at his side and returned to the Leopard House accompanied by many of the eunuchs. He died there two months later when he was only 31.

Zhu Houzhao, the playful and willful emperor the Great Ming Empire, passed away without a son or daughter. His death also marked the beginning of the gradual decline of the Ming dynasty.

"A Wonder in the World," inscribed on the name sign of the wooden pagoda at Yingxian in Shanxi Province by Emperor Zhengde in his own hand.

Inside the Yongling area.

Yongling

Four persons, an emperor, an empress and two imperial concubines were buried in Yongling. Construction of the tomb started in 1536 when Zhu Houcong, the 11th emperor of the Ming dynasty, was still alive. It is the largest of the 13 Ming tombs (occupying 250,000 square meters of grounds). Because the deceased emperor had no offspring, the traditional custom of "the younger brother succeeding the elder brother" was followed and Zhu Houcong, the emperor's cousin, succeeded to the throne and stayed in it for 45 years. As the son of a prince, he was unsure of himself and felt that he did not have a firm foothold in court. He was suspicious, acted arbitrarily and led a life of dissipation. All his actions revealed a paranoiac streak.

Court Officials Are Dismissed in a Great Debate; The Emperor Gathers Followers and Confers Title on His Father.

Zhu Houzhao, or Emperor Zhengde, died of illness

Yongling.

in the Leopard House on the western outskirts of Beijing on the 14th day of the third month in the 16th year of Zhengde (1521). As he had no son or brother, traditional customs required that a successor was to be found among the collateral relatives of the imperial family. With the empress dowager and court officials working together, Zhu Houcong, Emperor Hongzhi's nephew and Zhu Houzhao's cousin, was chosen to succeed to the throne when he was 14 years old.

Zhu Houcong, born in 1507 in Prince Xing's Mansion in Anlu, Hubei, was taken to Beijing from Hubei and became the new emperor on the 22nd day of the fourth month. He was known as Emperor Jiajing in history. Following the feudal traditions of succession, the empress dowager and court officials arranged to have Zhu Houcong adopted to become a brother of Zhu Houzhao. His uncle, Zhu Houzhao's father, became his father and his own father became his uncle. But Zhu Houcong was strongly against this arrangement.

Six days after ascending to the throne, he ordered the Board of Rites to call a meeting of senior officials to give his deceased father an honorable title and memorial ceremony. What he wanted was that since he had become the emperor in Beijing, his father who died in Hubei should also be honored as an emperor instead of being treated as a prince. As the senior officials disagreed, a "great debate on the question of ceremony" ensued.

On the 25th day of the ninth month in the same year, Zhu Houcong took his mother Lady Jiang to Beijing. Since her title had not been decided on, she stayed in Tongzhou on the outskirts of Beijing. The new emperor declared that if his mother was not given an honorable title, he would abdicate and return to Hubei with his mother. Empress Dowager Zhang and the senior officials had no choice but to change Lady Jiang's title from Concubine of the Prince of Xingxian to Empress Dowager Xingxian. Mother and son were thus able to stay together in the palace.

After several years of manipulations, Zhu Houcong gradually appointed a number of officials who supported him in Beijing. The honorable title of his father was changed to Emperor Gongmuxian, the Natural Father, and that of his mother, to Empress Dowager Zhangsheng, the Natural Mother. Those who opposed him in the past were imprisoned, had their salaries reduced or sent home. In the seventh month of the third year of Jiajing (1524), Zhu Houcong again decided to remove the "natural father" in his father's title because it hinted that he had been adopted by his uncle. This was again opposed by some officials. Kneeling on the ground, 229 officials petitioned outside the Zuoshun Gate of the palace, requesting the emperor to take back his decision. Seeing that his position as the emperor had been consolidated, Zhu Houcong started a mass slaughter. Eight of the leaders of the officials were imprisoned first. Then 134 of them who refused to withdraw were also locked up. Altogether more than 180 of the officials were punished by flogging with a big stick, and 160 of them were beaten to death on the spot, before the incident of kneeling petition was wholly suppressed. The emperor's father was posthumously given the title of Emperor Xingxian; his mother, Empress Dowager Zhangsheng; his uncle Zhu Youtang, Emperor Uncle; Empress Dowager Zhang, Empress Aunt. Zhu Houcong thus rearranged his relationship with the former emperor. Through the "great debate on the question of ceremony," he succeeded in driving away the former imperial forces represented by the family of Empress Dowager Zhang out of the circle of power. The young emperor from the outside of Beijing eventually was able to hold his ground in the capital.

A Tomb Patterned on Changling Is Built; It Exhausts the People and Drains the Treasury.

When Zhu Houcong began to think of building his tomb long before his death is not known. When

Carved stone at Yongling.

Surface tower in the snow.

Empress Chen died in the seventh year of Jiajing (1528), he took the opportunity to select a site for a tomb. The officials he sent out to find a site had chosen two places and drawn detailed pictures of them. When the pictures were presented to him for his decision, he was only 22.

At spring blossoming time in the 15th year of Jiajing (1536), the emperor, accompanied by the empress dowager, empress, concubines and a large entourage, came to the Heavenly Longevity Mountain tomb area. Besides offering sacrifices to ancestors, the purpose of the visit was to choose a site for his own tomb. Assisted by geomancers, he made an on-the-spot investigation and chose a place called Hill of Eighteen Ridges. When construction started on the 22nd day of the fourth month, he personally attended the commencing ceremony after offering sacrifices to Heaven and Earth. For the construction of the tomb, 40,000 soldiers of the Ming army were drafted to help in the work in addition to the countless number of corvée laborers engaged in quarrying, firing bricks, lumbering and transport.

For the scale of the tomb, Zhu Houcong decreed, "The style of the tomb should be patterned on that of Changling, but reduced in scale." But in actual work, no official dared to change the size. With the emperor's personal participation, besides reducing the size of the sacrificial hall from one of nine bays to one of seven bays, the scale of every structure was larger than the tombs of all the former emperors. After three years of intensive work, the Board of Rites and Board of Works reported in the seventh month of the 18th year of Jiajing: "The tomb in the mountains has been completed." It was said that Zhu Houcong immediately went there to see it. Standing on the top of a hill, he asked the officials, "Is this my completed tomb?" What he said sounded that he was not satisfied with it. The officials hurriedly replied that an encircling wall has to be built. As a result, in addition to the wall of the tomb, another encircling wall was built outside it. A sacrificial kitchen and storehouse and two long lines of buildings like those in the palace were added inside the encircling wall. The finished tomb occupied 250,000 square meters of grounds.

The tomb built before the emperor's death was not only large in scale, but also built with the finest construction materials, better than any one of the tombs of the former emperors. Most of the bricks for building the tomb came from the kilns in Linqing Prefecture, Shandong. Each of the bricks weighed about 20 kilograms. There were strict demands on its quality. It must "chime when knocking on it and be without pores when broken into halves." The qualified bricks were then allowed to be loaded in boats to be shipped to the capital. To ensure the quality of the bricks, each one was impressed with words like: "Made by so-and-son of the so-and-so kiln assigned by the manufacturing supervising official of the Lingqing kilns on certain day and certain month in the 15th year of Jiajing." It seemed that a system of personal responsibility was already in practice in those days.

The marble and green stone for the

Portrait of Emperor Jiajing.

Handwriting of Emperor Jiajing.

construction of the tomb were quarried from prefectures and counties near Beijing. But the hard granite had to be shipped from Junxian County in Henan, 500 kilometers away. The large quantities of building materials were transported by boats to Tongxian, east of Beijing, and then over land to the construction site. Under the transport conditions in those days, it was a strenuous task. It took altogether eight years to complete the tomb of Zhu Houcong.

The Emperor Is Misled by Heretical Taoist Priests; He Dies in Pursuit of Immortality.

Although Zhu Houcong was young, he was obsessed by divination and superstitious heresies after becoming the emperor. Misled by the eunuch Cui Wen, he set up Taoist altars everywhere in the palace to burn incense, worship Taoist deities and burn magic incantations to pray for longevity. A Taoist named Shao Yuanjie from the Dragon and Tiger Mountain, one of the places of origin of Chinese Taoism, was said to have immense magic power and be able to talk to deities in Heaven. Zhu Houcong believed it and invited him to the palace to perform Taoist rituals. Blindly trusted by the emperor, Shao was later promoted to the post of President of the Board of Rites and became leader of Taoism in the whole country.

Catering to the emperor's likes, some officials often bribed the Taoist priests to speak to the emperor about "auspicious" signs. One of them lied that the Yellow River had become clear, which promised the emergence of a sage in the peaceful and prosperous world. The emperor soon sent a high official to offer sacrifices to the River God. Another one presented to the emperor a white deer, saying it was an auspicious creature, for which the emperor went personally to the ancestral temple to pray. Later, such things as a giant ganoderma and a wheat stalk with three ears on it were presented to the emperor. The donors were rewarded or appointed to high official posts. In the emperor's later years, someone secretly put two fresh peaches on the throne and said that they were rewards from Heaven. For that, the emperor went to the Hall of Supreme Ultimate to express gratitude. These things showed how foolish the emperor had become as a result of his obsessive superstition.

Zhu Houcong believed in pills of immortality, which would enable him to live for ever. Supervised by Shao Yuanjie, the so-called "immortal lead pills" were produced in the 19th year of Jiajing (1540). The pills were said to have been made of herbs and some minerals, mainly mercury, mixed with the first menstrual discharge of young maidens. For the production of immortality pills, several batches of young girls from eight to 14 were summoned by decree to the palace for continuous supply during the reign of Jiajing. There were from more than 100 to as many as 300 girls in each batch.

Shao Yuanjie's pills of immortality eventually gave the emperor his quietus. In the 45th year of Jiajing (1566), the emperor became swollen all over. As no doctor could cure him, he died in the Western Garden outside the palace.

The Emperor Is a Suspicious and Peevish Man; He Is Nearly Strangled by Angry Palace Maids.

Zhu Houcong, who had succeeded to the throne as a collateral relative of the imperial family, had no roots in Beijing. He was psychologically on guard against all those around him as soon as he became the emperor. As he was a narrow-minded person in nature, those who submitted to him prospered and those who resisted him perished during his 45 years of reign. Many of the things he did revealed his paranoiac tendency. Many of the high officials who disobeyed him were beaten to death, imprisoned or exiled to the frontier regions. Crafty persons who catered to his whims were promoted. It was said that during his reign, more than 200 persons in the rear quarters of the palace were put to death for their mistakes. As he swallowed pills all the year round, the palace maids became sex objects for satiating his carnal lust. Overcome with fear, hatred and disgust and unable to endure it any longer, the palace maids decided to brave death and fight back on the 21st day of the 10th month in the 21st year of Jiajing (1542).

In the depth of the night, while Zhu Houcong was sleeping in the hall of Lady Cao, the Rui Concubine, 16 palace maids headed by Yang Jinying, after careful planning, slipped into the hall and decided to put the emperor to death. As they had planned beforehand, some of them covered the emperor's head with a yellow silk scarf, others tied his hands and feet, two of them tied a rope around the emperor's neck to strangle him. In a hurry, the two who tied the rope around his neck made a fast knot instead of a slipknot. Although they tried to tighten the knot for a long time, the emperor fell into a swoon but did not die. One of the maids cowered out of fear and reported to the empress of what was happening. People immediately came to save the emperor, who did not come out of his coma until the following afternoon after emergency treatment. The 16 palace maids, both the principals and accomplices, were executed by slowly slicing to death. Their families and relatives in other places were also put to death. Empress Fang took this opportunity to have the emperor's two favorite imperial concubines, Cao and Wang, killed on the excuse that they failed to report what was happening. Zhu Houcong could do nothing about it at the time, but he held a grudge against the empress because he missed his two favorite concubines.

Throughout Chinese history, no precedent can be found of defenseless women challenging a feudal emperor at the price of their lives. After the incident, Zhu Houcong did not dare to live in the palace any longer. He moved to the West Garden, where, hoodwinked by Taoists like Shao Yuanjie and Tao Zhongwen, he continued to swallow pills and pray for a long life and believed that it was the kindness of Heaven and Earth that saved him from death during the incident. Drawing a lesson from what had happened, he selected girls from eight to 14 in age to serve him, not only for obtaining ingredient for making pills, but more importantly for safety. He lived in the West Garden for more than 20 years and rarely ventured out until he died and was carried back to the palace by eunuchs.

Zhaoling

Buried in Zhaoling are Zhu Zaihou (1537-1572), the 12th emperor of the Ming dynasty, and three women, who were:

Lady Li was wife of the Prince of Yu before the prince became the emperor. She was given the title of empress after her death, and later reburied in Zhaoling in the ninth month of the sixth year of Longqing (1572).

Lady Chen was the second wife of the Prince of Yu. When Zhu Zaihou mounted the throne, she be-

A distant view of Zhaoling.

came the empress. When she died of illness in the seventh month of the 24th year of Wanli (1596) at the age of 56, she was buried in Zhaoling in the ninth month of that year.

Lady Li, the natural mother of the emperor, died in the second month of the 42nd year of Wanli (1612) at 70. She was buried in Zhaoling in the sixth month of the same year.

Superstitious Belief Separates Father and Son; The Prince Lives Away from the Palace for 13 Years.

Emperor Jiajing stayed in the throne for 45 years.

Blank stele pavilion at Zhaoling.

Front gate of Zhaoling.

For the purpose of having more offspring, he had made 81 women his empresses and concubines. But these women gave birth only to eight sons, and six of them died when they were still young. Only the third and fourth sons survived.

At first, Zhu Houcong was in a hurry to make his first and then his second son the crown prince. But both of them died young. A superstitious rumor began to spread in the palace that two dragons could not see each other. If they met, one of them would be hurt. Since the emperor was believed to be the incarnation of a dragon, his sons and grandsons were certainly also dragons. Obsessed by the heretic Taoist sayings, Zhu Houcong stopped conferring the title of crown prince to any one of his sons and even refused to see them. In the 32nd year of Jiajing (1533), the 16-year-old Zhu Zaihou was made the Prince of Yu and ordered to marry. The wedding ceremony was supposed to be held in the palace. But Zhu Zaihou was strongly against it. The wedding eventually took place in the mansion of the Prince of Yu outside the palace. Although Zhu Zaihou was the legitimate successor to the throne, he was not given the title of crown prince and lived a quiet and independent life.

During the 13 years while Zhu Zaihou lived in the mansion of the Prince of Yu, his father never summoned him to his presence. As Zhu Zaihou lived away from the smoldering strife of the court and the struggle in the rear quarters of the palace and influenced by several of his teachers when he was young, he had opportunities to come into contact with all kinds of people in society and understand the condition of the ordinary people.

An interesting thing happened after Zhu Zaihou had ascended to the throne. One day, he wanted to eat sweet sesame cakes and ordered a eunuch to pre-

The Inner Red Gate.

Lingen Hall.

pare some. The victualling supervisor and the pastry kitchen of the emperor quickly made a list of ingredients required, such as sugar, flour, pine nut kernels and hazelnuts, for making sweet sesame cakes at the total cost of several thousand ounces of silver. Looking at the list, the emperor smiled and said: "Sweet sesame cakes can be bought at Goulan Street off Chang'an Boulevard at half an ounce of silver for a whole box. Why do you need so much money?" Failing to cheat the emperor, the eunuchs timidly withdrew. This happening showed that Zhu Zaihou was an upright and kind person.

But Zhu Zaihou did not become an enlightened ruler because by nature he loved a life of pleasure and dissipation. As he indulged for a long period in sensual pleasure, his health was seriously compromised. He died only six years after ascending to the throne.

Two Girls Come from Two Different Families; They Later Become Two Empress Dowagers.

More than 400 years ago, there lived a Chen family and a Li family in Yongledian Village, Tongzhou, on the outskirts of Beijing. The Chen family's ancestral home was in Jianzhou of the Northeast, the birthplace of the Nüzhen people. Because their fore-father had been re-warded for his mili-tary exploits and became a heredi-tary captain of the army, the whole family moved to Tongzhou and had,

Sacrificial vessels and objects in the Lingen Hall.

by the middle period of the Ming dynasty, become a well-to-do scholarly family. The Li family had for generations lived in Tongzhou and earned a living by farming and as a builder of houses to make up the deficiency. The two families were vastly different in their economic conditions, but they had one thing in common. Each of the families had a girl of about the same age. The girl of the Chen family was a sensible young lady of considerable learning. The girl of the Li family, because her family was poor, worked as a maid in the Chen family. Free from many worldly prejudices, the two girls, a master and a servant, became as close as two sisters.

In the fourth month of the 37th year of Jiajing (1558), Lady Li, wife of Zhu Zaihou, the Prince of Yu, died of illness. Recommended by local government officials, the daughter of the Chen family was chosen and became the second wife of Zhu Zaihou. The 13-year-old daughter of the Li family also went to the mansion of the Prince of Yu as the Chen girl's maid. In the first year of Longqing (1567), when Zhu Zaihou succeeded to the throne, the Chen girl was made his empress. History books say that Empress Chen "had no sons and was often ill." The fact was that as Zhu Zaihou indulged in sensual pleasure and entrusted all government affairs to court officials, Empress Chen often advised him against it and aroused the emperor's displeasure. The emperor found an excuse and sent Empress Chen to live in another palace.

After moving into the mansion of the Prince of Yu, the girl from the Li family grew up and became a pretty young woman. She was intelligent and comprehending and favored by Zhu Zaihou, who made her his imperial concubine when the Chen girl was made the empress. Li gave birth to two sons and two daughters. Her second son was Zhu Yijun, who later succeeded to the throne and became known as Emperor Wanli.

In the sixth year of Longqing (1572), the 36-year-old Zhu Zaihou passed away as a result of "drinking long into the night" and "indulging in sensual pleasure." His second son succeeded to the throne. His natural mother, Imperial Concubine Li, and his adoptive mother, Empress Chen, were both promoted to become empress dowagers. As Chen was a kind-hearted woman, Li treated her with respect just as before. The existence of two empress dowagers together was a rare situation in the history of the Ming dynasty. As Chen lived in the Ciqing Palace, and Li in the Cining Palace, they were known as "empress dowagers of the two palaces" and well spoken of by people both inside and outside the palace.

Flaming Arch.

A Virtuous Official Encourages Thrifty Spending; Approved by Empress Dowager, an Old Tomb Is Put to Use.

On the 26th day of the fifth month in the sixth year of Longqing (1572), Zhu Zaihou died after a long illness in the Qianqing Hall of the palace when he was only 36 years old. In the memorial on the construction of the emperor's tomb, Zhang Juzheng, an official of the cabinet, and Feng Baocan, a senior eunuch of the Department of Rites, wrote: "The tomb should not be simply and thriftily, nor extravagantly and wastefully built." The meanings of the words canceled each other in what they wrote. Since the new emperor

Surface building.

was only 10 years old and could not take part in government affairs, and the two empress dowagers were not in a position to intervene, the funeral of Zhu Zaihou was to be handled by court officials. The famous minister Zhang Juzheng volunteered to take up the responsibility.

In the memorial on the construction of the tomb, Zhang Juzheng, the leading official of the cabinet, who had already a plan in mind, wrote that the Underground Palace that had long been completed at the foot of Dayu Hill in the tomb area could be put to use as the tomb of Zhu Zaihou. This bold proposal of his aimed at saving a great deal of money and lightening the work of the laborers. Zhu Heng, the President of the Board of Works, who was to oversee the construction of the tomb, also wrote a memorial, in which he glorified the Underground Palace at Dayu Hill, saying that there were purple rays of good luck and peaceful atmosphere in the Underground Palace, where the chambers are clean and warm like sitting-rooms. The two empress dowagers were very pleased and agreed to their proposal.

The origin of the Underground Palace could be traced back to 35 years before. In the 17th year of Jiajing (1538), when Zhu Zaihou was only one year old, his grandmother, Lady Jiang, died in Beijing. The reigning Emperor Zhu Houcong intended to ship the coffin of his grandfather (Emperor Xingxian) to Beijing to be entombed together with his grandmother. A tomb site

A wax likeness of Zhu Zaihou, Emperor Longqing, at Zhaoling.

was chosen in Changping and construction of the Underground Palace lasted more than a year. But later, after being pursued by court officials, Zhu Houcong changed his mind. In a decree, he explained: "I thought throughout the night about moving the coffin. Since my father has been buried for nearly 20 years, I feel uneasy to see it exposed to wind and dust during the long journey." He made a special trip to his birthplace at Anlu in Hubei to see his father's tomb. After comparing the two places, Zhu Houcong found that the mountains and rivers in Hubei were more elegant. So he ordered the surface structures at the tomb to be rebuilt in the style of an emperor's tomb. When he heard that there was probably water near the tomb, he had an underground palace built behind to tomb along the axis. After the reconstruction, the tomb eventually became an emperor's tomb surrounded by two circular walls. The tomb became known as Xianling. His mother's coffin was shipped under the escort of court officials down the Grand Canal from Tongzhou and then along the Yangtze and Hanshui rivers to Anlu in Hubei. As a result, the completed Underground Palace and the half-finished foundation of the surface hall were left unused in the tomb area in Changping.

Because much of the work for the construction of the Underground Palace had been completed, the construction of Zhu Zaihou's tomb was finished in a short time. All the surface structures were built in a year.

A bird's-eye view of Dingling.

Dingling

Dingling is the tomb of Zhu Yijun, the 13th emperor of the Ming dynasty, and his Empress Wang and Honorable Imperial Concubine Wang (Emperor Taichang's natural mother). Zhu Yijun succeeded to the throne at 10 and stayed in it for 48 years (1573-1620). In the first eight years, all court affairs, large and small, were handled by court officials in the name of the young emperor and under the supervision of Empress Dowager Li, the emperor's natural mother. During this period, the leading court official Zhang Juzheng carried out reforms in officialdom, finance and taxation and achieved successful results. Records show that the revenue of the Ming court increased steadily. There were 13 million hectoliters of reserved grain and seven million ounces of silver in the

Picture showing the original layout of Dingling.

treasury, which amounted to 10 years of government expenditure. Society and the economy also progressed rapidly in the stable political situation. When Zhang Juzheng died of illness in the 10th year of Wanli (1582), the power of government came into the hands of Zhu Yijun when he was just over 20. Suffering probably from psychological inhibition as a result of long years of disciplining by his mother and Zhang Juzheng, Zhu Yijun began to act willfully with the power in his hands in running the huge Central Empire.

With unlimited power in his hands, the first thing Zhu Yijun decided was the construction of his own tomb. Although it was beyond everybody's expectations, no one could disobey the emperor's order. After the completion of the tomb, Zhu Yijun never again stepped out of the palace again. In the 28 years from the 20th year of Wanli (1592) to his death in the 48th year of his reign (1620), he never made his presence at court and never held sacrificial ceremonies to Heaven and his ancestors. As a result, the days of the Great Ming Empire became numbered.

Main entrance to Dingling.

The Young Man Is Concerned About Things After Death; He Acts in Total Disregard of Ancestral Traditions.

With the supreme power in his hands, the first thing Zhu Yijun did was to mobilize people to build his tomb. One day soon after the Spring Festival in the 11th year of Wanli (1583), the 21-year-old young emperor walked leisurely into the office of the cabinet and informed the senior officials there that he intended to hold an ancestral memorial ceremony at the Heavenly Longevity Mountain on the Clear and Bright Festival and at the same time choose a site for his own tomb. Drawing a lesson from the confiscation of Zhang Juzheng's family properties after his death, none of the cabinet officials dared to offer outspoken advice. They suggested that some officials were to be sent out to choose several sites and draw pictures of them for the emperor to decide. With the participation of eunuchs from the Department of Rites, several officials and geomancers headed by Zhang Siwei, a member of the cabinet, scouted the entire tomb area and selected three possible sites. Two months later, in the intercalary second lunar month, Zhu Yijun went to see the three sites when he came to perform the ancestral memorial ceremony with his empress and imperial concubines. But he was not satisfied with any one of the three sites. Officials were again sent by the Boards of Rites and Works in the third month to choose new sites. Five sites were chosen this time. In the eighth month, the emperor ordered Xu Wenbi, the Duke of

Blank stone stele at Dingling.

Dingguo; Shen Shixing, the Grand Secretary; Zhang Hong, a eunuch from the Department of Rites, and some others to take the fourth trip to the tomb area to see the chosen sites. After repeated comparisons, two were chosen from the five sites for the emperor to make the final decision. On the Height-ascending Day of clear autumn sky and air at the Double Ninth Festival on the ninth day of the ninth month the following year (1584), the emperor went with a large entourage, including the two empress dowagers, empress, imperial concubines and a large number of officials, to the Heavenly Longevity Mountain tomb area in the name of holding an autumn sacrificial ceremony. With the approval of the two empress dowagers, Zhu Yijun eventually

Carved stone on the steps of the Lingen Hall.

chose a site on the same side of Xiaoyu Hill as his father's tomb, so that father, mother and son could care for one another in the nether world.

On the sixth day of the 10th month that year, the construction of the tomb formally began after a ceremony of offering sacrifices to Heaven and Earth. Zhu Yijun already had in his mind about the scale of his tomb. He issued a decree to the Boards of Rites and Works, ordering them to build his tomb on the same scale as Yongling, the tomb of his grandfather, Zhu

Houcong. Some officials advised against it, maintaining that it was inappropriate to build his tomb larger in scale than his father's tomb in the vicinity. But Zhu Yijun simply ignored the advice. In the course of construction, he came twice to the spot to check the progress and quality of his tomb. In the ninth month of the 16th year of Wanli (1588), he even made a special trip to the underground palace where he was to sleep for eternity. He was highly pleased when he saw that the entire tomb with high arch ceiling was built with huge blocks of stone and that the floor was paved with fine square stone tiles shining like black jade and the rear hall built with stones as colorful as a brocade. In his pleasure, he sat himself on the throne of carved marble and entertained himself with wine. After six years of painstaking work, the tomb covering 180,000 square meters of grounds was completed in the 18th year of Wanli (1590). It is recorded in history books that the construction cost eight million ounces of silver, the amount of two years of national revenue in the middle period of the Wanli reign. People in the past commented on the tomb appropriately, saying that "it exhausted the money of the inner court and the ingenuity of the builders."

Flaming Gate.

The Emperor's Favor Leads to Sorrow and Grievances; Lady Zheng Fails to Realize Her Fond Dream.

One winter day in the ninth year of Wanli (1581), Zhu Yijun had nothing to do in the rear quarters of the palace and came casually to the Cining Palace where his mother, Empress Dowager Li, lived. As his mother was not there, a palace maid named Wang who waited on him attracted his attention. The maid had a slim figure and a pretty face and gave clever answers to every question he asked. The young emperor was captivated and soon had sex with her. This kind of thing was too casual to be mentioned for an emperor in feudal society. The young emperor soon forgot all about it until one day in the fourth month of the following year (1582), while eating a meal with his mother, the empress dowager, said to Zhu Yijun, "The maid in my palace named Wang and favored by you has become pregnant." The news came so sud-

Wall surrounding the grave of Honorable Imperial Concubine Zheng.

denly that the emperor did not know what to say. He blurted out, "There was no such thing." The empress dowager ordered someone to fetch "The Daily Records of the Emperor's Life," which showed in black ink on yellow paper that it did happen. Instead of becoming angry, the empress dowager comforted the emperor, saying, "I am getting old and have not a single grandson. If the maid gives birth to a boy, it will be a blessing from our ancestors." She also instructed the emperor that the mother must be honored on account

Inside the grounds of Dingling.

Portrait of Zhu Yijun, Emperor Wanli, buried in Dingling.

of her son and that the woman named Wang should be treated properly. On the 16th day of the sixth month that year, Wang was conferred the title of Imperial Concubine of Gong. On the 11th day of the eighth month, Wang gave birth to a boy, the eldest son of the emperor, named Zhu Changluo.

At this time, the woman most favored by the emperor was Lady Zheng. Selected and brought to the palace in the ninth year of Wanli when she was 15, she was conferred the title of an imperial concubine of the fourth rank on the sixth day of the third month in the 10th year of Wanli (1582). She was given the title of an imperial concubine of the third rank when she became pregnant a year later and the title of an honorable imperial concubine after she had given birth to the second and seventh daughters of the emperor. In the first month of the 14th year of Wanli (1586), when Lady Zheng gave birth to Zhu Changxun, the emperor's third son, the emperor was exceptionally pleased. Soon after the baby was a month old, Zheng was made the first honorable imperial concubine, next in rank only to the empress. By comparison, the mother of Zhu Changluo, the emperor's eldest son, was left out in the cold without any hope for promotion.

The vastly different treatment to Zheng and Wang gave rise to widespread comments both inside and outside the court. People worried that the emperor might act against the ancestral traditions and appoint not his eldest but his third son as the crown prince. There were actually rumors among the public, saying that when the emperor and Imperial Concubine Zheng went to a Taoist temple to pray, they pledged in front of the statue of Lao Zi that the emperor's third son born of Zheng was to be appointed as the crown prince.

Portrait of Empress Xiaoduan.

For that, the emperor wrote a secret decree to be preserved by Zheng. Court officials had repeatedly requested the emperor to name the crown prince "in order to consolidate the foundation of the country." But the emperor simply ignored them. The naming of the crown prince was postponed again and again until the first month of the 29th year of Wanli (1601). When the emperor went to see his mother in the Cining Palace, the empress dowager asked him about naming his eldest son as the crown prince. The emperor said, "But the eldest son was born of a palace maid." His words greatly enraged the empress dowager, who said sternly, "You yourself was born of a palace maid." Realizing that what he had said had hurt his mother, he hurriedly knelt down, admitted his mistake and promised that he would immediately name the eldest son the crown prince.

When Zheng heard the news, she became very dissatisfied with the emperor. She hastily opened the jade box in which she had kept the emperor's secret decree that promised the appointment of the third son as the crown prince, so that she could argue with the emperor. It was probably the will of Heaven that the paper on which the emperor had written the secret decree had become worm-eaten and the words on it had become undecipherable. All Zheng's efforts to make her son the crown prince had come to naught. Zhu

Yijun had no alternative but formally to name his 19-year-old eldest son, Zhu Changluo, as the crown prince on the 15th day of the 10th month of that year.

After her son was named the crown prince, the plight of Wang, however, had not improved. She was conferred the title of an honorable imperial concubine in the 34th year of Wanli (1606) after the emperor's first grandson was born and after the emperor was urged by court officials. It was said the Wang lived in seclusion in a different palace all the year round and shed tears out of sadness all day long until her eyes could not see things. In the 39th year of Wanli (1611), when Wang was critically ill, the crown prince was permitted to see her. He found her palace gate locked and had to enter by breaking the gate. Mother and son cried together when they met. When Wang passed away in the ninth month of that year at 47, she was buried near East Well in the tomb area of Changping. Ten years later, when her grandson mounted the throne, she was moved to Dingling and given the title of Empress Xiaojing.

Marrying Off the Emperor's Daughter Is an Important Event; The Future Son-in-Law Is Selected from Behind a Curtain.

There was rigid stratification in feudal society. When doing everything, a person's social position and family background had to be taken into consideration. In marriage, the man's and woman's families must be well matched in social status. When the most lofty emperor was to marry off his

Portrait of Empress Xiaojing.

daughter, it was a spectacular event and the talk of the town. When a princess married, it was called "marrying down" or "lowering down," meaning that she was going down in social status. For the man's side, it was called "matching the so-and-so princess."

The emperor's son-in-law was called Fuma, literally meaning "side horse." His official title was "captain of the side horse," a name first used in the Han dynasty and was originally the title of an officer of the emperor's bodyguards. As a close relative of the emperor, the Fuma did not serve a substantial public office. Most of the Fumas in the Ming dynasty received salaries but did not occupy any government position. The purpose of this arrangement was to prevent the Fumas from bullying people by flaunting their powerful connections, gaining profits through the powers in their hands and thus compromising the name of the Imperial House. A few of them were assigned to work at the Court of the Imperial Clan (an office for handling the register and affairs of the imperial clan), where they did the routine work, such as making copies of documents. But the Fumas received favorable political treatment. When there were large-scale political activities, such as celebrations and court ceremonies, the emperor's sons-in-law were positioned among the distinguished relatives of the emperor when civil and military officials lined up on the eastern and western sides of the court.

The selection of a Fuma was carried out under the direction of the emperor. The Board of Rites would put up a notice for selecting a husband for a princess, stating that the sons and brothers of government officials in the capital or of military men and civilians who were 14-16 in age, regular in appearance, well-behaved and properly brought up could apply. If no suitable candidates could be found in the capital, the area of selection would be extended to the counties and prefectures around Beijing or even to Shandong and Henan. As the saying goes, "The emperor's daughter needs not worry about finding a husband," every time such a notice was posted, hundreds or even thousands would apply. Some even bribed officials and eunuchs to be selected.

When the local governments received the list of candidates, officials were sent out to check on the candidates' family background, personal reputation, whether they had any bad habits and whether any member of the family in three generations upwards had malicious disease. The results of the check were reported to court. Eunuchs from the Department of Rites were then dispatched to the various places to hold interviews with them one by one. Those who were too tall or too short, too fat or too skinny were eliminated. After several selections, some outstanding ones with handsome features, a good figure and free from gambling, drinking and other bad habits and deformity and with a better education were assembled for the chief eunuch, women officials in the palace and women members of the imperial clan to choose two or three from among them. The personal data of these young men would then be handed to court for the emperor, empress, empress dowager and others to choose the successful candidate.

After the successful candidate had been decided on, he was sent to the Academy (the national highest institution of learning) to study for half a year, known as "learning the rites." He was to study and familiarize himself with the etiquette of the court and officialdom. At the same time, he should perform some elaborate ritual formalities, such as "asking her name," giving gifts and deciding on the date of the wedding, before he was to marry the princess. The Imperial House also gave gifts, or a dowry, to their daughter, which included not only jewelry, clothes and other things, but also land and estates. It is recorded in history books that when Zhu Yijun married off his younger sister, Princess Shouyang, the bride was given 1,395 *qing* (39,373.8 acres) of land, and Princess Shouning born of Honorable Imperial Concubine

Five stone sacrificial vessels in Dingling.

Zheng was given 2,590 *qing* (42,667.66 acres) of land. This may explain why so many people were eager to marry a princess.

In the 27th year of Wanli (1599), on the day when the emperor was to choose a husband for Princess Shouning born of Honorable Imperial Concubine Zheng, both the emperor and Zheng sat behind a curtain to choose their future son-in-law. There were three candidates. Two of them named Gu from the capital. When they came to the palace, both were carefully decked out. It was a hot summer day. Dressed in formal clothes, both had a big pin of white jade in their hair and carried a sachet at the waist, which emitted a sweet smell around them. The third candidate was name Ran, from Gu'an in Hebei. He was simply dressed in ordinary clothes and wore a round hat. When he came into the palace, he "kowtowed gingerly and did not dare to look up." After a discussion, the emperor and Zheng chose the simple country young man, Ran Xingrang, to be their son-in-law.

Most of Fumas chosen by the Ming Imperial House were from commoner families. This was because they did not have extravagant desires and easy to control. The marriage, the relation between husband and wife, was not necessarily a happy one. Princess Rongchang, the eldest daughter of Zhu Yijun, was married to Yang

Chunyuan. The relation between husband and wife was a spiteful one. One day, incited by the princess, Yang was beaten by a number of palace maids. Having no place to complain, he ran back to his own home in the country. When

Entrance to the Underground Palace of Dingling.

the emperor learned about it, he had him sent back by the local government and forced him to study ritual in the Academy for half a year as a punishment. Although he was beaten and punished for the wrongdoing of the princess, he had no place to argue his case in the Imperial House.

Dingling Is Excavated After Three Diggings; What Happened in History 400 Years Ago?

For historical research, a committee for the excavation of Changling formed by scholars and specialists was established with the approval the State Council in the 1950s. But in the course of actual survey, the committee found that Changling is very large in scale and requires some experience before it could be excavated. So the committee requested approval for the trial excavation of Dingling instead.

Dingling was built during the reign of Zhu Yijun, or Emperor Wanli, on the model of his grandfather's tomb, Yongling. Construction started in the 12th year of Wanli (1584) and completed six years later in the 18th year of Wanli (1590). After completion, the tomb was covered with earth for later use. Thirty years later, when Zhu Yijun died after a long illness in the Dehong Hall of the palace on the 21st day of the seventh month in the 48th year of Wanli (1620), he was to be buried together with his Empress Wang who had died in the fourth month and whose coffin was in the rear quarters of the palace, and Honorable Imperial Concubine Wang, the crown prince's natural mother. The first

Plan of the Underground Palace:
1. Diamond wall.
2. Vestibule.
3. Front chamber.
4. Middle chamber.
5. Rear chamber.
6. Left side chamber.
7. Right side chamber.

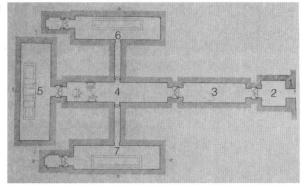

thing the new emperor, Zhu Changluo, did was to perform elaborate funerals and bury his father, the empress and his natural mother together in Dingling. Without anybody expecting it, Zhu Changluo died from a sudden illness only a month after succeeding to the throne. The funerals and burial were to be handled by his son Zhu Youjiao. It was unprecedented in Chinese history to have two emperors lying in state together and waiting to be buried. The national treasury at the time was almost empty and the political situation was in confusion. Faced with the chaotic mess, the 15-year-old young emperor was unequal to

the tasks and at a loss what to do. As a result, the funeral and burial of the emperor Zhu Yijun and his two wives were hastily performed in confusion. History books say that the coffins of Zhu Yijun and Empress Wang began to be moved from the palace to the tomb area on the 28th day of the ninth month that year. More than 8,000 soldiers and civilian laborers were

Tunnel gate.

mobilized to move them. Because the coffins were very heavy, it was very difficult to move them. The thick wooden sticks and ropes broke several times. It took a whole day to move the coffins to the Victory Gate of the city wall. The soldiers and laborers were reinforced by 600 more men to move the coffins out of the city the following morning. On the way, a large wooden stick broke and caused one corner of the emperor's coffin to hit the ground. When they reached Gonghua Town, the emperor's travel lodge in Shahe, it was already midnight. When people began to settle down for the night, it was time to perform the ceremony of offering wine and fruit to the dead. The master of ceremony shouted many times but received no answer. This showed how confusing the command and administration of the funeral had become. After the coffins of the emperor and his two wives were placed in the underground palace on the third day of the 10th month, the gate of the tomb was closed and the tunnels leading to it were filled with earth. Trees were planted to make it look just like before.

The trial excavation of Dingling commenced 336 years later in May 1956. For archaeological study, the excavation of the tomb was to be carried out as scientifically as possible. From known data obtained from on-the-spot surveys, some bricks had subsided at the southeastern side of the encircling wall, revealing signs of an arch gate built of bricks. After study, it was decided first to dig a ditch of 3.5 meters wide and 20 meters long from the corresponding side of the encircling wall. A stone slab carved

Granite tablet indicating distance to the tunnel.

with the words for "Tunnel Gate" was soon discovered on the inner side of the encircling wall. Shortly after digging farther, two walls built of large bricks were exposed. The two walls formed a tunnel of eight meters wide, winding its way in an S towards the surface tower on the axis. This was the tunnel through which the coffins of the emperor and his wives were taken to the underground palace. To reduce the amount of digging, a second deep ditch was dug crosswise behind the surface tower. When the ditch was 7.5 meters deep, a granite tablet was found inscribed with the words: "This stone is 16 *zhang* [53.4meters] from the front side of the diamond wall and 3.5 *zhang* [11.7 meters] deep." This discovery created a stir at the site. After an analysis, it was believed that the stone was a marker placed there for diggers to reach the tunnel. There were two reasons for the stone tablet to show the way to the underground palace. 1. Dingling was built and buried underground for future use. There was no fixed date for its use and no one knew how long it would be before it was put to use. It was, therefore, reasonable to leave a marker to facilitate the smooth opening of the tunnel. 2. There was no fixed number of the emperor's wives to be buried with the emperor during the Ming dynasty. There were instances of opening the tunnels again and again for the burial of empresses and imperial concubines who died later than the emperor. It was reasonable to leave a marker.

Following leads provided by the inscription on the granite tablet, a third longitudinal deep ditch was dug. As the digging progressed, archaeologists found that where they were digging was a long tunnel built of mottled stone. The tunnel sloped downwards to a brick wall at the end. The wall was nine meters high and

Removing bricks of the diamond wall during the digging.

Objects in the middle chamber as they were found during the digging.

The rear chamber when it was opened.

The Underground Palace of Dingling.

An "automatic stone" for buttressing a gate from the inside.

decorated with yellow glazed tiles at the top. This was the diamond wall. (In ancient Chinese architecture, an inside wall was called diamond wall, meaning it was as strong and unbreakable as a diamond.) Measured with the measures of Ming architecture, the distance between the stone tablet and the wall was exactly the distance indicated by the inscription on the stone tablet.

Some of the bricks of the diamond wall facing the tunnel had inclined inward as a result of earth rammed from above it. There were signs of patching up of the wall. When these bricks were removed, the opening led to a vestibule with an arched roof, a transitional structure leading to the underground palace. The arched roof is 7.3 meters from the floor. At the end of the vestibule was a huge marble gate tightly closed and buttressed from inside with stone slabs. This was the gate of the underground palace that had been buried for nearly 400 years.

After a year of work, people had at last stood at the threshold of revealing the many secrets of the underground palace.

The Emperor's Inner Palace Has Many Halls and Chambers; The Underground Palace Boasts Beamless Buildings.

The underground palace of Dingling has five chambers: front, back, middle, left and right. The gen-

The marble throne, five sacrificial objects and a blue-and-white jar with oil and wick in it to provide a long-burning lamp of the dead in the middle chamber.

eral layout was patterned on the emperor's inner palace. The ancient belief that "The dead is to be served as the living" was embodied in the construction of the tomb. The entire underground palace was built of stone with arched roofs and measured 76 meters in length and 1,195 square meters in floor space. It is a group of beamless buildings.

The underground palace has seven gates. The three on the axis are the most exquisite. Each leaf of the marble double gates is 3.3 meters high and 1.7 meters wide with 81 studs on it, the sum of nine multiplied by nine, a number that stood for the emperor who was the highest in rank. Each side of the double gates was carved with a whole stone. The upper end of the hinge is cylindrical and the lower end, semispherical.

The hinge side is 40 centimeters thick and becomes thinner on the other side, where it is only 20 centimeters in thickness. This design not only reduced the weight of the gate, but also ensured the solidity of the hinge. The nearly four-ton gate can be opened and closed without much effort. Rumors said that there were poisoned arrows and traps in the underground palace to prevent robbery. Excavation showed that there were no such devices. All the tightly closed seven gates were buttressed from inside with stone slabs. Following the instructions in history books, archaeologists made a key with a bent head, inserted it into the crack between the two leafs of the double gate, prodded loose the stone slabs and opened each of the gates. After opening the first gate, people found there were words written in ink on a slab of stone, which said, "All the automatic stones of the seven gates have been examined." The stone slabs were called automatic stones because a stone slab was placed in a sloping position on the inside of the gate and when the gate was closed it automatically slid down and buttressed the gate.

The back of the throne is carved with a dragon design.

The read chamber of the Underground Palace.

Inside the underground palace, the front and middle chambers are paved with "golden tiles," a kind of finely made floor tiles from Suzhou in the south. There were also pieces of square wood on the floor, which were probably placed there to prevent damaging the floor when the coffins were being moved in. The reason why they had not been removed afterwards is not known.

The front chamber is 20 meters deep, six meters wide and 7.2 meters high without anything in it. Scattered on the floor were some jade beads and pearls. They must have come off from the covering of the coffins.

The middle chamber is 32 meters deep and the same in width and height as the front chamber. There are three tables of carved marble positioned there in the shape of an A. These are altars of the emperor and empresses. In front of the altars are five sacrificial apparatuses (two candle seats, an incense burner and two vases). There is also a large porcelain vat inscribed with words for its manufacture during the Jiajing years of the Ming dynasty. The vat is 0.7 meter in its mouth diameter and 0.8 meter deep. The oil in it and the floating wick show that it is the long-burning lamp for the dead. Perhaps it was not probably designed. As there was still a great deal of oil in it, it did not burn very long before it went out.

Passage leading to a side chamber.

Both the left and right side chambers are 26 meters in width, seven meters in depth and 7.4 meters in height. There is a flat platform in the middle of each of the chambers for placing a coffin. There is a rectangular hole at the center of the platform with yellow earth in it. The hole is known as the "golden well." The ancients believed that the hole allowed the "ground vapor" to come in from the outside, so that the dead could be in touch with and in harmony with Nature. There is a stone door at the end of each of the side chambers. The door is supposed to open to a tunnel, but there is no tunnel. As there are nothing else in the two side chambers, they were built there as parts of the design of an emperor's tomb.

The rear chamber of the underground palace is much larger than the other chambers. It was 30.1 meters wide, 9.1 meters deep and 9.5 meters high. The floor is paved with tiles of mottled stone shipped from faraway places. In the middle of the rear part is a large coffin platform with the coffins of the emperor

and two empresses on it. Around the platform are pieces of fragrant wood from the South Seas and Hetian jade from Xinjiang. The rest of the space is occupied by 26 large boxes painted in red and fully loaded with burial objects. The secrets that had been buried underground for nearly 400 years were at last disclosed.

A side chamber.

Notes on the Artifacts Unearthed

All the Land Under the Sky Belongs to the Emperor; There Is Gold Everywhere in the Imperial Palace.

More than 3,000 artifacts have been unearthed from Dingling. Most of them are articles for everyday use by the emperor and empresses, such as gold and silver ornaments and jewelry, belts and ribbons, silk and embroidered clothes. Some of them have been unearthed for the first time in China. These artifacts are of very high value.

In the Ming dynasty, there were two silver workshops in Beijing and Nanjing, where a number of highly skilled artisans were assembled to make continually all kinds of objects for use in the palace. To show his kindness, the emperor gave these objects as gifts to his favorite court officials, members of the imperial clan and heads and envoys of foreign countries. The objects were made with the best material and the finest craftsmanship in the silver workshops.

A hat, known as the winged crown, was found in Zhu Yijun's coffin. The whole hat was woven with fine

Winged crown woven with fine golden filaments.

Winged crown of dark gauze.

golden filaments, weighing 826 grams. Each of the holes is hexagonal in shape like the structure of a beehive. The skill with which the hat was woven is a marvel. On the top of the hat are two lively dragons toying with a pearl woven with multiple golden filaments. The hat is the only one of its kind to be found in China. History books say that when Zhu Yijun was taking a rest or at play in the rear quarters of the palace, he liked to wear a hat of golden filaments inlaid with pearls and jewels. When he was pleased, he would give this kind of hat to a eunuch close to him.

Gold, as a precious metal, was used to show the lofty status of the imperial clan and nobles. During

A formal headgear.

Wine pot of pure gold.

Gold plate decorated with dragons toying a pearl.

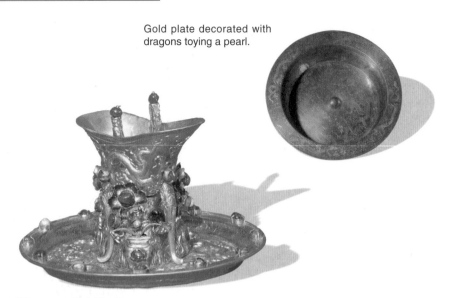

Wine vessel inlaid with precious stones.

Gold wine pot inlaid with precious stones and carved with dragon designs.

the Ming dynasty, repeated orders were issued prohibiting the use of gold by the ordinary people. The several hundred pieces of jewelry and ornaments and a large number of bottles, vases, wine cups, basins, plates, bowls and chopsticks were made with a large quantity of gold and often inlaid with precious stones of all colors. Most of the precious stones came from Burma, Thailand and even from Adan (today's Aden) in Central Asia. Among them, the cat's eye and emerald are the most precious and were purchased at high prices from various places for use in the palace. It is recorded in history books that a single cat's eye the size of a bean cost 1,000 ounces of silver. Another winged crown unearthed from Dingling is inlaid with more than 10 cat's eyes.

The Emperor Represents All the Admirable Virtues; His Rights and Wrongs Are Judged by Later People.
— Note on the Kesi Robe with Twelve Designs

The imperial robe was a ceremonial garment worn by the emperor only during the enthronement and important sacrificial ceremonies to Heaven and Earth. It had a history of more than 2,000 years. Although changes had been made during the different dynasties, the 12 designs on it had remained basically the same.

The imperial robes found in Dingling were woven, embroidered or made by the Kesi process. Those made with the Kesi process with 12 designs on them are the most gorgeous. They were not only made with the finest material (gold thread and thread made with peacock feathers), but also woven with the most diffi-

A Kesi robe with 12 designs on it.

cult skills, which involved a great deal of hard work.

Kesi is a very special method of weaving silk fabrics. The designs are woven with wefts of many colors on the warps. While the warps run through the length of the fabric, the wefts do not. This method of weaving, therefore, is called "whole warps and broken wefts." The technique was perfected during the Song dynasty (960-1279). The designs produced during those days were mainly Buddhist images and pictures of flowers and birds. As the work was wholly

Jade waist belt buckle.

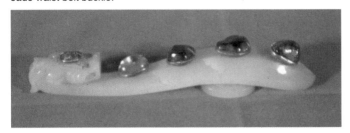

done by hand, efficiency was very low. It was said that it took a whole day for a worker of considerable skill to weave one square inch of design.

Each of the 12 designs embroidered on the emperor's imperial robe has its meaning and represents the emperor's virtue and integrity:

The sun, moon and star designs on the left and right shoulders and the back of the robe mean that light coming from the universe represents the emperor's boundless benevolence covering the whole world.

The mountain design symbolizes territorial integrity, the state and the dynasty, meaning that the dynasty would last for ever and be passed down to thousands of future generations.

The dragon was a primitive totem of the Chinese people. It was a deified divine creature "able to grow and contract in size, to bend or extend, to appear and disappear and to create cloud and rain." The ancients looked upon the emperor as the embodiment of the all-capable dragon. Each of the Kesi imperial robes

Belt with golden ornaments inlaid with emerald.

The empress's crown unearthed from Dingling is decorated with
three dragons and six phoenixes.

unearthed from Dingling is decorated with 12 designs of coiled dragons on the left and right sides and the front and back of the robe. The dragons are embroidered with special threads made of peacock's feathers, which shine with brilliant colors in the light.

The five-colored pheasant means that the emperor not only excelled in personal cultivation and literary talent, but also possessed the Five Constant Virtues of love, justice, propriety, wisdom and sincerity. He was, therefore, a perfect man.

The wine vessel is decorated with a tiger and a long-tailed monkey. The ancient people believed that the two animals were intelligent creatures who understood the need to distinguish the noble and the lowly and show respect to the senior. They mean that the emperor respected Heaven and his ancestors, followed closely the ancestral rules and was outstand-

Wine vessel of jade with a golden support decorated with a design of longevity hill and sea of blessing.

ing in filial devotion.

The millet grains symbolize that food was the most important need of the people. They express the wish for abundant harvests and the emperor's concern for the hardships of the people.

The fire flame means that the emperor provided warmth for the common people.

The waterweed shows that the emperor was to devote all his heart to the people and be just and honorable and uncontaminated by temptations.

The axe stands for the emperor's resolute decisions in handling affairs and willingness to listen to advice.

The double bows stand for the emperor's ability to make a clear distinction between the true and the false, detect the minute details and distinguish right and wrong.

By assigning all the lofty virtues on the emperor with the 12 designs, people expressed their expectations of the emperor and their wish for a good life. But no one knew what Zhu Yijun was thinking when he put on the robe.

Brooch inlaid with cat's eyes.

The Mother Is Honored Because of Her Son; The Baby's Clothes Are Pitiable Mementoes. – Note on Baby's Clothes in the Coffin

During the excavation of Dingling, three baby's coats were found in the coffin of Empress Wang, the natural mother of Zhu Changluo. All the three coats were made with plain woven gauze. Two of them had no decoration at all. The third one was printed all over with red bird designs. The bird, called Di in ancient times, was a long-tailed pheasant with multicolored feathers that represented talent and personal cultivation. The design was favored by empresses, imperial concubines and princess in the past. They liked to wear clothes with Di designs both in ordinary days and during a ceremony to show their lofty position and beauty.

A coat (replica) embroidered with the images of 100 babies unearthed from Empress Xiaojing's coffin.

Brooch made in the shape of the Chinese character for "heart."

Why were baby's clothes found among the burial objects in Empress Wang's coffin? It was deduced that the whole story must be like this: On the sixth day of the seventh month in the 12th year of Wanli (1584), Wang gave birth to the emperor's fourth daughter. The young princess, however, did not live long. She died of illness on the 25th day of the fourth month in the 15th year of Wanli when she was not yet three.

Earrings of jade rabbits.

After conferring the posthumous title of Princess Yunhe on her, she was buried at the foot of the Golden Hill in western Beijing. Although Wang had given birth to the eldest son of the emperor, she was discriminated against by Imperial Concubine Zheng. After the death of the young princess, she became more unhappy in the rear quarters of the palace. It was probably then that she kept some of her daughter's clothes as mementoes.

Zhu Changluo, the emperor's eldest son, was also discriminated against in both the rear quarters and the Eastern Palace. For years, mother and son could not even see each other. It was recorded that because Wang missed her son and daughter so much, she was unhappy all the time and pulled down by illness. Later, she even lost her eyesight. When she died in the ninth month of the 39th year of Wanli (1611) at 47, her baby's clothes were placed in her coffin probably

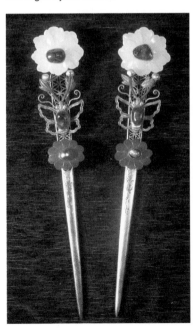

Hair pins with butterfly and flower designs.

Hair ornaments.

because some people in the palace sympathized with her or because of her last wish. The three pieces of simple clothes were saturated with a mother's profound love for her children.

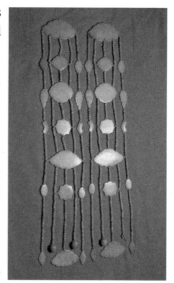

Jade pendants.

Magic Herbs and Elixirs of Life Are Offered to the Emperor; Court Physicians Swallow Medicine Before the Emperor.
– Note on the Long-handled Medicine Pot

Among the objects found in Dingling were two gold pots, each with a lid and a long handle. The bottoms of the pots were carved with the words: "Made during the Wanli reign of the Great Ming for imperial use with 85 percent of gold, weighing 22 ounces and four drams." (The actual weight is 895 grams.) Carved on the side of the pot are four words in double lines, meaning "For use by the emperor according to ancestral rules." The two pots were for boiling herbal medicines when the emperor was ill.

To ensure the emperor's access to medical

Gold medicine pot with a long handle.

attention, an imperial hospital was established near the palace, where a number of well-known doctors took turns to go on duty day and night and waited to be summoned to the palace to give treatment to members of the imperial clan by feeling their pulse and writing out prescriptions. The Inner Affairs Department in the palace had a pharmacy supervised by a senior eunuch and operated by 50-60 court eunuchs and medical doctors, whose job was to purchase the necessary medicines, prepare and take care of them.

When the emperor was ill, imperial doctors were summoned to the palace by order from the inner court. Four or six doctors would then be led by an official of the imperial hospital to the palace together with an

Blue-and-white porcelain vases.

official from the imperial pharmacy, all dressed in "auspicious cloths." Before entering the hall where the emperor lived, they all had to step over a fire pan with atractylodes and other fragrant herbs burning in it to rid themselves of "evil vapor" from the outside both in winter and summer.

Upon seeing the emperor, they kowtowed first and began to feel the emperor's pulse while kneeling on the floor. Two of the doctors formed a team to feel the emperor's pulse at his left and right wrests respectively and then repeat the process after exchanging their positions. After feeling the pulse, they reported their diagnosis based on the emperor's pulse conditions to the emperor. When the emperor agreed with their diagnosis, they would all withdraw to a side hall to prepare a prescription through discussion. The name, nature and quantity and of each of the ingredients as well as the way of preparing them were to be written out and presented to the emperor. The prescription was then taken to the imperial pharmacy to be dispensed.

Two portions of the prescription were prepared under the watchful eyes of an official of the imperial hospital and one from the inner court, and then placed together in a gold pot. After closing the lid, a yellow strip of paper with the words "The emperor's medicine carefully sealed" written on it was stuck on the pot. After boiling, the liquid was poured into two containers. The imperial doctors and the official from the inner court were to drink the liquid in one of the containers. When there was no bad aftereffect, the other container was taken to the emperor for his use. Finally, the date, the names of those participated in the treatment were written on the prescription, affixed with seal and stored away "for later examination."

Facts proved that serving as an imperial doctor was not a cushy job. If the emperor happened to die after the treatment, the imperial doctors were blamed for it and became scapegoats. Several unjustly charged cases had occurred during the Ming dynasty.

Porcelain wine vessel.

Qingling

Built in 1621, Qingling is the tomb of Zhu Changluo, the 14th emperor of the Ming dynasty, and his four wives. Zhu Changluo was in the throne only for a month before he died of illness and did not have the time to name his empress. Three of his wives were conferred the title of imperial concubine posthumously and reburied in Qingling afterwards. The three of them were:

Lady Guo married Zhu Changluo when he was the crown prince. The emperor Zhu Yijun reluctantly agreed to the marriage only after repeated urging by court officials. As the crown prince was already 21 years old, it was a late marriage according the customs at the time both among the common people and in the imperial family. Three years after the wedding,

Lady Guo gave birth to a daughter, who died prematurely. When Lady Guo died a sudden death at 21 in 1613, her father-in-law refused to decide where she was to be buried. Her burial was postponed repeatedly until three years later when she was buried in an ordinary place. She was reburied in Qingling as the empress only when Zhu Changluo died of illness four years later.

Emperor Taichang who was in the throne only for a month.

Ruins of the foundation of the Lingen Hall at Qingling.

Lady Wang was originally a waiting maid in the Eastern Palace where Zhu Changluo lived as the crown prince. She gave birth to the crown prince's first son in 1605. When the birth of her baby was reported to the palace, Zhu Yijun expressed no pleasure at all at the birth of his eldest grandson. It was the empress dowager who was exceptionally pleased by the arrival of her great grandson. For the birth of the baby, Lady Wang was conferred the lowly title of "junior concubine." When she died of illness at 30 in 1619, her coffin was deposited in a temple. As the palace was in utter confusion at the time, nobody cared about her burial. It was only when her son Zhu Youjiao mounted the throne as Emperor Tianqi in 1621 that she was buried as an empress in Qingling. The mother was honored because of her son.

Lady Liu was 10 years younger than Zhu Changluo. She gave birth at 18 to the emperor's fifth son and died in 1614 when she was 23 years old. She was buried at first at the foot of the Golden Hill on the western outskirts of Beijing. When Zhu Youjian succeeded to the throne after the death of his elder brother and became known in history as Emperor Chongzhen, the coffin of Lady Liu, his natural mother, was moved to Qingling as empress dowager.

A Strange Incident Occurs in the Palace; Scapegoats Are Put to Death.

In the 29th year of Wanli (1601), with the repeated urging and intervention from Empress Dowager Li, the emperor's grandmother, Zhu Yijun, the emperor, very unwillingly made his 19-year-old first son the crown prince. At the same time, he made his third son, Zhu Changxun (born of Honorable Imperial Concubine Zheng), the Prince of Fu, and his fifth son, Zhu Changhao, the Prince of Rui. According to the Ming dynasty's political system, when a prince came of age, he must leave the capital and go to his fiefdom. This was known as "going to the fiefdom." Without court decree, he was not allowed to leave his fiefdom and come to Beijing. The original purpose of this arrangement was to prevent brothers fighting for the throne in the capital. When some court officials saw that the Prince of Fu's long stay in the capital was not good for the crown prince, they proposed that the Prince of Fu must leave immediately for his fiefdom in Luoyang. Honorable Imperial Concubine Zheng was the first person against it. Behind her was the emperor, Zhu Yijun. As a result, the Prince of Fu's departure for his fiefdom was postponed again and again until the 42nd year of Wanli (1614) when Empress Dowager Li died and the Prince of Fu was deprived of his excuse of staying in the capital to celebrate the birthday of his grandmother. It was only then that the Prince of Fu left Beijing with a large amount of gifts and his overstay for 13 years in the capital came to an end.

After the death of the empress dowager, the crown prince, Zhu Changluo, lost his only guardian in the rear quarters of the palace. The following year (1615), the "clubbing incident" which aimed at murdering the crown prince shocked the court and the country as a whole.

On the night of the fourth day in the fifth month, when things had quieted down in the capital and inside the palace, a burly man suddenly appeared at the Eastern Flowery Gate of the palace. Armed with a club of jujube wood, he swung it against anyone who happened to be in his way. He rushed into the palace and headed straight north for the Ciqing Hall where the crown prince lived. The old eunuchs who guarded the door were beaten to the ground because they were no match for the man. When the man fought his way to the door of the hall, several guardian eunuchs came to the scene and arrested him.

As the incident was a serious one, it was handed over to the Board of Punishments. After questioning, the man was found to be named Zhang Chai, who lived in Tongzhou to the east of Beijing and made a living by delivering firewood to several brick kilns. At the time, Honorable Imperial Concubine Zheng was financing the construction of a temple with bricks and tiles from these kilns. One day, two eunuchs, named Pang Bao and Liu Cheng, serving Zheng came to Zhang Chai and asked him if he wanted make a fortune and told him if he could kill Zhu Changluo, the crown prince, he would be given 30 *mu* (five acres) of land so that he would be able to live comfortably for the rest of his life. On the fourth day of the fifth month, the two eunuchs took Zhang Chai to a big house outside the

Chaoyang Gate of the city (a house belonging to Pang Bao outside the palace) and served him a rich meal. Afterward, Zhang Chai was given a thick club of jujube wood and led to the Eastern Flowery Gate of the palace. The incident of breaking into the palace and clubbing people then took place.

The incident incited heated controversy both inside and outside the court, which affected the judgment of the case. Some people maintained that Zhang Chai was a lunatic and what he said could not be true. Others believed that there must be a plotter behind Zhang Chai and a thorough investigation must be made. As the latter's opinion prevailed, the development of the case made Honorable Imperial Concubine Zheng extremely nervous. She insisted that the emperor should make the final decision. To alleviate the situation, Zhu Yijun asked Zheng to go to the Eastern Palace and tell the crown prince that she was innocent.

The Inner Red Gate.

Seeing his step-mother crying, the crown prince changed his attitude. Instead of saying that "there must be a plotter behind Zhang Chai," he, together with his father, the emperor, explained to the court officials that they must not force him to act unfilially. Zhu Yijun also told the court officials that the whole imperial family was living in perfect harmony. As a result, Zhang Chai was put to death by dismemberment for "lunatically breaking into the palace" and the two eunuchs serving Zheng were beaten to death. The "clubbing incident" was thus brought to an end. But later people looked upon the case as one of the three most doubtful cases at the end of the Ming dynasty. No final conclusion about the case has been reached even today.

The Emperor Is Overcome by Sorrow and Weariness; A "Red Pill" Sends Him to the Other World.

On the 21st day of the seventh month in the 48th year of Wanli (1620), Zhu Yijun, or Emperor Wanli, who had stayed in the throne the longest among all the emperors of the Ming dynasty, passed away after illness. On the first day of the eighth month, Zhu Changluo, the crown prince, eventually ascended to the throne and became known in history as Emperor Taichang. From the day he was born, Zhu Changluo had been discriminated against and left in the cold. As a result of long years of tension and repression, he was harmed both physically and mentally. He had nothing to do in the Eastern Palace before. But as soon as he had succeeded to the throne, a great number of disorderly affairs were placed before him and waited for him to deal with. The funeral and burial of his father, step-mother and natural mother had to be arranged immediately. Although his first wife Guo and Junior Concubine Li (natural mother of Emperor Tianqi) had died long ago, they had to be conferred the title of empress because they had served him for many long years. His step-mother Zheng made every effort to draw Lady Li, a favorite concubine of Zhu Changluo, to her side, and the two joined hands in demanding to be conferred the titles of empress and empress dowager. All this kind of things dazed and exhausted the new and not very brilliant emperor. In addition to family affairs, state affairs were even more upsetting. Nurhachi, a tribal leader of Liaozuo in the Northeast, had proclaimed the founding of the Later Kin dynasty four years ago to rival the Ming court. As his father had imposed exorbitant taxes and levies on mines and salt production, people were forced to rise in revolt in many places. It was by adopting some good ideas worked out by court officials that the extremely urgent troubles were obviated. He had, for example, twice allotted 1,600,000 ounces of silver to provide food and clothing for soldiers fighting on the Liaozuo front, issued decrees to withdraw all officials in charge of collecting salt taxes, and recalled all the officials who had been punished and sent to work in the frontier areas for holding different opinions during the Wanli reign. The emperor's new policies and measures gave people hope that things might become better.

As the saying goes, "A good thing is always accompanied by setbacks." Only four days after Zhu Changluo's ascendance to the throne, a rumor began to spread, saying that the emperor was ill. Based on

Stone columns of the Flaming Gate.

the rumor, court officials began to write memorials to the emperor, advising him "to take care of himself in his daily life, to preserve his vital energy, to control his sensual desire, etc." The advice was not totally groundless. It was said that to curry favor with the new emperor, Honorable Imperial Concubine Zheng gave him four beautiful women (Another version says there were eight.) Although this could not be the cause the emperor's illness, the court officials insisted on finding the cause of his illness. Zhu Changluo had no choice but to explain. He said that he had caught cold in the Eastern Palace and had not recovered completely from it. As there were now the funerals of his father and mother and elaborate rituals, he was overcome by sorrow and fatigue. About his symptoms, he said that he felt dizzy and powerless in his limbs. When the court officials saw that the emperor was only eating less and coughing, they concluded that he could not be seriously ill.

On the 14th day of the eighth month, a eunuch named Cui Wensheng brought medicine to the emperor. Cui was a eunuch from Honorable Imperial Concubine Zheng's palace. After Zhu Changluo mounted the throne, Zheng recommended him to serve as the secretary of the Department of Rites and thus became the first secretary of the emperor and a close aide. He also served as the superintendent eunuch of the imperial pharmacy. It was said that instructed by Zheng, Cui gave the emperor a medicine composed mainly of rhubarb, which caused diarrhea. The emperor had go to the toilet 30 to 40 times in a day and night and was confined to bed. When the emperor's condition became known, court officials demanded that the misuse of medicine should be linked with Honorable Imperial Concubine Zheng, and

Cui Wensheng and the plotter behind him should be punished accordingly.

Before this trouble was over, an official named Li Kezhuo from the Department of Rites said that he had a wonder medicine that could cure the emperor's disease. When he was summoned to the palace, he offered a red pill, which the emperor swallowed in front of court officials at noon on the 30th day and the eighth month. The emperor soon declared that he felt "warm and refreshed" and "had an improved appetite." The red pill was said to have been made with menses discharge mixed with ginseng and deer antler and was a powerful tonic. In the evening, the emperor worried that the pill might have exhausted its potency. He asked for another pill from Li Kezhuo and swallowed it. When the court officials saw that the emperor was quite well, they stopped worrying and returned home. The following morning, news of the emperor's death was announced and shocked everybody.

Besides answering the question of whether the emperor was killed by the two red pills, the "case of red pills" intensified the factional struggles in the court and hastened the downfall of the Ming empire. Nobody seemed to care about the investigation into the "case of red pills." Only Cui and Li were sent to a frontier area for penal servitude. Zhu Changluo became the shortest reigning emperor in the history of the Ming dynasty.

Deling

A portrait of Emperor Tianqi in the sitting position.

Deling, built in 1627, was the tomb where Zhu Youjiao, the 15th emperor of the Ming dynasty, was buried with his Empress Zhang. In the ninth month of the 48th year of Wanli (1620), the 15-year-old Zhu Youjiao succeeded to the throne as the eldest son of the emperor and became known in history as Emperor Tianqi. After becoming emperor, Zhu Youjiao, like his father, also faced with insolvable troubles in state and family affairs. The chaotic state of things his father did not have time to deal with was left to the young successor. As a common saying goes, "One stops worrying when there are too many debts and does not feel itchy when there are too many lice." When Zhu Youjiao found it was beyond his ability to deal with the hopeless mess of things, he adopted an attitude of doing nothing and left all government and family affairs to his trusted eunuchs and court officials, while he himself lived in a quiet place, doing nothing and seeking after only his personal pleasure.

Zhu Youjiao stayed in the throne seven years (1620-1627). One day, he "felt not quite himself" and then "becoming increasingly edematous." He passed away after a few month when he was only 22.

The Emperor Leaves State and Family Affairs to Others; With Manual Dexterity, He Becomes a Skilled Carpenter.

After two emperors had died of illness in 40 days, history placed the supreme power of a big country in the hands of Zhu Youjiao, a 15-year-old boy and the eldest grandson of Emperor Wanli. It was indeed a big joke played on people by Heaven. A boy without a proper education and nearly illiterate suddenly became the ruler of a country. Faced with the mess left behind by his father, the boy was at a loss what to do. He became less worried only when he thought about a person he could trust. This person was Wei Zhongxian, a eunuch who was a cook in the Eastern Palace and had been with him for 15 years.

Wei Zhongxian had been a rogue in the street, who had a wife and a daughter. After he had gambled away all his belongings, he voluntarily performed castration, became a eunuch and came to the palace during the Wanli reign to serve as a meal attendant for Junior Concubine Wang, Zhu Youjiao's natural mother. Wei was a man of powerful build and a glib talker. Although he was illiterate, he had a very good memory and a remarkable ability to get along with people. Wang had given birth to the emperor's eldest son, but she was not favored by the emperor and quite straitened in circumstances. It was Wei who did everything possible to enable mother and son to live a comfortable life. It was said that Zhu Youjiao disliked reading books and was restless and loved to play since his childhood. To cater to the boy's likes, Wei taught him to play football and chess and keep birds and crickets for fighting and won the boy's trust. Wei was also a skilled cook. The clams, prawns, frog legs, young chicken breasts and a mixed strew of sea cucumber, abalone, shark's fin, chicken and pig's trotter Wei prepared were the boy's favorite since childhood. Wei's seemingly "unlimited ability in doing everything" fascinated the young Zhu Youjiao, who began to make an idol of him. As soon as he ascended to the throne, he promoted Wei to the position of a secretarial eunuch of the Department of Rites and superintendent of the Eastern Chamber (a spy agency). As the young emperor was ignorant of and not interested in power, he handed over all the complicated political affairs to Wei, who acted on behalf of the emperor

A panoramic view of Deling.

and became the most powerful figure in court next only to the emperor.

It was recorded in history books that Zhu Youjiao was "extremely versatile and dexterous with his hands and most interested in building construction." Together with some young eunuchs, he built miniature palaces with wood, complete with halls and pavilions. on an empty lot in the palace. He wielded the adze, chisel, axe and saw and painted and decorated himself. His skills in carving and cutting "were so perfect that even an experienced artisan's work could not compare with his." The miniature palaces were built and pulled down repeatedly, but he was never tired of it.

Some old eunuchs in the palace recalled that Zhu Youjiao had made some amusement devices by installing mechanism in a wood barrel or brass vat. When the barrel or vat was filled with water, the water flew down and became a fountain or waterfall. A specially made wooden ball rolled up and down in the water. Both the design and craftsmanship were highly ingenious. When Zhu Youjiao was immersed in it, "he would forget to eat and did not feel hot or cold when the weather changed." It was said that at an occasion like this, Wei Zhongxian would take an important document to the emperor for approval. The emperor had no interest in the matter and would say offhandedly, "You handle it yourselves. I know about it." Wei was thus able to carry out his own decisions by relaying a verbal message of the emperor. This gradually led to the monopolizing of power by the "eunuch clique" at the end of the Ming dynasty.

After several years of operation, Wei Zhongxian enlisted many followers and placed his trusted men inside and outside the court, who formed a clique. People at the time described the key figures in the clique as the "five tigers, five young tigers, 10 dogs and 40 siblings." The monopolizing of power by the eunuch clique accelerated the fall of the Ming dynasty.

A Fight for "Companion" Breaks Out in the Palace; The Emperor Passes Judgment on a Strange Case.

Eunuchs were castrated men who had lost the male sexual function and were chosen to serve the emperor and his family in the palace. As these men lived close to the emperor, they often became the emperor's most trusted persons to rely upon. Although there were strict regulations preventing eunuchs from interfering with government affairs, the regulations were often overlooked.

Wei Zhongxian came to the palace in the 17th year of Wanli (1589) when he was 21. He worked at first as a storehouse keeper and later made friends with another eunuch named Wei Chao. Through him, Wei Zhongxian became the meal attendant of Junior Concubine Wang, the natural mother of Zhu Youjiao. The two eunuchs were so close to each other that they became sworn brothers.

There was a very strange phenomenon in the Ming palace. If a eunuch and a palace maid found each other congenial, they could form a pair like husband and wife to look after each other in their daily life so as to make up their spiritual void and satisfy their physiological urge. Such pairs were known as "companions." It is recorded in history books: "There were hardly anyone without a partner in the palace. The partners lived

The snow-covered Inner Red Gate.

just like husband and wife. When they decided to marry, they made pledges under the moon and stars, vowing never to love another."

Wei Chao had come to the palace early and had already formed a pair of "companions" with Ke, the wet nurse of Zhu Youjiao. Ke had been married and given birth to a daughter back in her native place. She was summoned to the palace at 18 when Zhu Youjiao was born. After Wei Zhongxian became Junior Concubine Wang's meal attendant, he often played with the boy Zhu Youjiao during his leisure and came to know Ke. Wei was 20 years older than Ke, but the difference in age did not prevent them from getting together. As Wei Chao often went out on official business, Wei Zhongxian took the opportunity to replace him and became very close to Ke. "The magpie's nest was occupied by the turtledove," as the saying goes.

After Zhu Youjiao became emperor, his wet nurse Ke continued to look after him in his daily life in the rear quarters of the palace. Late one night when Wei Zhongxian and Ke were making love in a side room of the Qianqing Palace, Wei Chao caught them when he returned from an errand outside the palace. The two Weis called each other names and then came to blows. The noise disturbed Zhu Youjiao in the main hall. A guardian eunuch brought the two to the emperor. But after listening to their complaints, the emperor could not make a decision. He sent for Ke and asked her to decide. Ke was straightforward and said that she would like to become "companions" with Wei Zhongxian. The emperor decided immediately. He sent Wei Chao away and helped Wei Zhongxian and Ke to become "husband and wife."

Shortly afterwards, the emperor dismissed Wei

Chao and sent him to his native home in Fengyang. Wei Zhongxian secretly had him killed on the way. Later, Ke was conferred the title of Emperor-serving Lady and Wei Zhongxian promoted to the position of secretarial eunuch of the Department of Rites. Both thus became very powerful persons in the palace during the Tianqi reign.

The Emperor Puts Up Notices to Choose a Wife; The Unhappy Empress Zhang Is Victimized.

In the 11th month of the first year of the Taichang reign (1620), after Zhu Youjiao had ascended to the throne for more than two months, Sun Ruyou, President of the Board of Rites, wrote a memorial, saying that the emperor was almost 16 and should marry. The memorial was quickly approved. The Board of Rites then put up notices announcing the selection of girls between 13 and 16. Those who passed the preliminary selection were taken to Beijing at government expenses. Because the imperial decree said that "the wedding should take place immediately and selections made at prescribed time," more than 5,000 girls were taken to Beijing by their parents three months later in the first month of the first year of Tianqi (1620). This was the largest selection for a wife in the history of the Ming dynasty.

In Beijing, the girls stayed at guest houses (usually for receiving foreign envoys) and the 10 princes' mansions. On the day of selection, the girls were lined up, according to age, in groups with 100 girls in each group. Eunuchs sent by the palace looked at each one of them. Those who were too tall, too short, too fat or too thin were eliminated. "More than 2,000 of them were sent back." The second careful selection was made several days later, and the girls were also lined up with 100 in each group. This time the selectors looked at the girls' facial features according to the standard set in the book *Ma Yi Shen Xiang* on physiognomy used by fortune tellers. Those whose ears, nose, mouth, eyes and color of hair and skin did match the descriptions in the book were eliminated. Only 800 girls remained after the second selection. In the third selection, the girls were to tell their name, age and place of birth. Those who could not speak clearly or their voice was coarse or unpleasant were out. After the three selections, only less than 300 remained. Several more selections were made to look at their hands, feet, the way they walked and if they had scars on their bodies. By the third day of the fourth month, only eight girls had the honor of attending the final selection in the Yuanhui Hall of the palace by the empress, imperial concubines, women court officials and senior eunuchs. Three of the best were chosen to stay in the palace waiting to be conferred imperial titles. They were Zhang from Henan, Wang from Shuntian Prefecture of Beijing, and Duan from Nanjing. The five others were "sent home." Enthusiastically urged by Liu Kejing, chief eunuch of the Department of Rites, the wedding took place on the 27th day of that month. The 14-year-old Zhang was made the empress, and the two others, imperial concubines.

Empress Zhang, named Zhang Yan and pet named Baozhu, was born of unknown parents. Her foster-father was a poor scholar. One day, when he went out to collect rents for others, he saw an abandoned baby in the snow and took it home. That day, the sixth day

Stone columns of the Flaming Gate and surface building.

of the 10th month in the 35th year of Wanli (1607), became the birthday of Empress Zhang. As the common saying goes, "A child in a poor family learns to look after household affairs when he or she is very young." Zhang was a diligent and sensible girl and able to do all the house work even when she was young. Her foster-father gave her an education in history, literature and general knowledge. An old eunuch recalled that "She had firmness of character and liked to read and write."

In the palace, Empress Zhang was disgusted with Ke and Wei Zhongxian's domineering attitude. She had complained to the emperor and warned Ke to her face, but to no avail. Ke and Wei therefore hated her and were afraid of her. They found an excuse to send Liu Kejing, the eunuch who supported Empress Zhang,

Gate of the tomb administration department of Deling.

into exile and then had him killed.

In the third year of Tianqi, Empress Zhang was pregnant. Ke and Wei worked hand in glove and transferred all the palace maids not friendly to them away from the Kunning Palace and replaced them with those who were their followers. One day, the empress had a back pain. Ke and Wei instigated the maids to give her a forceful massage, which led to a miscarriage.

In the eighth month of the seventh year of Tianqi (1627). Zhu Youjiao died and was succeeded by his fifth brother Zhu Youjian, who honored his 20-year-old sister-in-law as Empress Yi'an, meaning Empress of Fine Virtue, treated her with courtesy and found a place for her in the rear quarters of the palace. In the third month of the 17th year of Chongzhen (1644), the insurgent peasant army led by Li Zicheng captured Beijing. Empress Zhang fled from the palace in the confusion and was found by Li Yan, one of the leaders of the insurgent army, who sent her back to her foster-father's home. Seeing that both her country and home were ruined, she committed suicide by hanging herself when she was 37. When the Qing army came to Beijing, they buried her in Deling together with Zhu Youjiao. Empress Zhang eventually rested in peace after a lifetime of frustrations.

Siling

Siling is the tomb of Zhu Youjian, the 16th emperor of the Ming dynasty, and his Empress Zhou and Honorable Imperial Concubine Tian.

In 1644, when the insurgent peasant army seized Beijing, Zhu Youjian hanged himself on the Longevity Hill behind the palace. As he had not built a tomb for himself, he was temporarily buried in the graveyard of Honorable Imperial Concubine Tian, who died of illness a few years before.

A sitting portrait of Emperor Chongzhen.

Purging the Eunuchs, the Emperor Tries to Revive the Dynasty; Acting Too Hastily, He Fails to Employ the Right People.

Zhu Youjian came to the throne when the Ming regime was in troubled times. The peasant resurgent army had occupied the Northwest and the southern half of the country; Huangtaiji in Shengjing (Shenyang) was amassing a big army ready to take

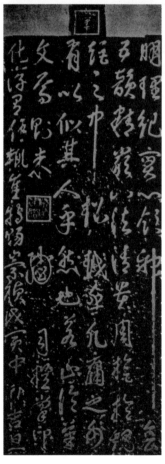

Emperor Chongzhen's handwriting.

over the Central Plains; the court officials had divided into factions engaged in grim struggles. All the important government departments were controlled by the followers of Wei Zhongxian. It was said that when the completely isolated Zhu Youjian came to the palace on the 23rd day of the eighth month, he could not sleep all that night. As there was no one around him who could be trusted, he had to take a sword from a patrolling eunuch for the night to defend himself. He also remembered the warning given him by his sister-in-law, Empress Zhang, not to eat anything prepared in the palace and eat only the griddled cakes he had brought with him. It was after the succession ceremony that he managed to bring eunuchs and maids from his former Prince Xin's mansion to the palace and began to feel safer.

There is an ancient Chinese saying: "Every new sovereign comes with his own courtiers." Zhu Youjian knew he had many things to do, such as recovering the lost territories in Liaodong, suppressing the insurgent army and readjusting the appointments of officials of the cabinet. But the most urgent task was eliminating the eunuch clique. Since Wei Zhongxian's followers were everywhere, Zhu Youjian had to protect himself first and wait for an opportunity. After mounting the throne, he treated the eunuch clique with unusual

Stone tablet at the surface building of Siling.

tolerance and patience at first.

To find out which way the wind was blowing, Wei Zhongxian made the first probing move six days after Zhu Youjian ascended to the throne. He handed in his resignation to the emperor. The emperor did not approve his request to resign and said some nice words to ask him to stay. A few days later, Wei proposed that the construction of shrines in memory of his birth in the various places should stop. The emperor tactfully agreed but added that those that had not been built should stop and those that had been completed should stay. Not long afterwards, the emperor issued three iron tallies to Wei's sons and nephew exempting them from death punishment for three kinds of offence in order to show the preferential treatment given to them. After a month of observation, the Wei clique began to rest assured that everything would be all right.

Biding his time, the emperor waited for an opportunity to take action. The opportunity came as a result of plotting and intrigue within the Wei's clique. In the middle of the 10th month, the die-hard followers of Wei Zhongxian handed in a memorial exposing Cui Chengxiu, the President of the Board of War, for forming a faction and taking bribes. This, however, made Wei lose face. Zhu Youjian took the opportunity to have Cui dismissed and threw the whole political situation off balance. A turn of the sensitive political weathercock encouraged many of the court officials, who came forward in large numbers to expose and condemn the eunuch clique. The emperor called Wei Zhongxian to his presence and asked someone to read the memorials. Wei had no choice but to resign on the excuse of being ill. Zhu Youjian approved his resignation and sent him to look after the ancestral tomb (the tomb of Zhu Yuanzhang's parents). On the way to the tomb, when Wei heard that the emperor was going to arrest and punish him, he committed suicide. The news of his death made both the officials and common people happy beyond themselves and their cheers resounded like peals of thunder. The eunuch clique was dealt a fatal blow.

In the face of difficulties both internally and externally, Zhu Youjian was determined to resurrect the dynasty created by his ancestors. But as he was young and arrogant, acted with undue haste and was oversimplified, crude and suspicious in appointing people to their jobs and in carrying out administrative measures, he alienated himself from the court officials and the people. Statistics show that in the 17 years while he was in the throne, he reappointed 43 presidents of the Board of Rites and changed 17 presidents of the Board of Punishment, two of them being executed. Because of setbacks in war, seven commanders at the front were beheaded and had the bodies displayed in a marketplace, and 11 provincial governors were killed. In the 12th year of Chongzhen (1639), when the Qing army intruded into this side of the Great Wall, he blamed the officials at the front and executed 36 of them in one day. Among the officials who participated in court affairs, he had 50 of the Grand Secretaries removed one after another. As the situation became increasingly more difficult, the sovereign and court officials were unable the exchange views. Zhu Youjian muttered continually, "I am not the ruler of a fallen country, but everything indicates the doom of the country." What he said shows that Zhu Youjian was unwilling to allow his country to fall into ruins, but could do nothing about it.

In the fourth month of the ninth year of

Chongzhen (1636), Huangtaiji founded the Great Qing State in Shenyang and exerted tremendous pressure on the Ming dynasty. Directed by the emperor, Chen Xinjia, President of the Board of War, sent a secret envoy with the emperor's edict to the Qing army to negotiate for peace. The envoy had made several trips, but no agreement could be reached. When the news of the peace negotiation became known, Zhu Youjian denied it to save his own face. In the seventh month of the 15th year of Chongzhen (1642), Chen Xinjia was executed for colluding with the enemy. For the unsuccessful peace negotiations and defeat in war, Zhu Youjian continued to blame others. Even before his death, he still said, "The court officials failed me."

The Insurgent Army Lays Siege to the Capital; The Emperor Is Deserted by the People and Officials.

On New Year's Day in the 17th year of Chongzhen (1644), Li Zicheng declared himself a king in Xi'an, founded the state of Dashun and set up government offices. On the 11th day of the first month, the Board of War in Beijing received a letter of challenge to war delivered by a messenger sent by Li Zicheng. The letter of challenge was like an ultimatum. It stated that the insurgent army was to fight a decisive battle with the Ming army by the city wall of Beijing. When the news about the letter was passed on to the emperor, the emperor was at his wits' end. The scholar Li Jiantai, who was serving as the Grand Secretary, came forward and volunteered to lead a western expedition to

Shanxi to stop the insurgent army's attack. The emperor was highly pleased. A sending-off ceremony of the highest standard was held on top of the Zhengyang Gate Tower, where the emperor personally gave a sword representing dedicated power and farewell wine to Li. But before Li marched very far out of the city of Beijing, news of defeats in the battles in Shanxi reached him. Not daring to proceed, he held the army there and waited. The noisy fuss of the sending-off ceremony fizzled out like a farce.

In the second month, the emperor issued a decree, ordering all the army units in the various places to come to the capital to defend the city and protect the imperial family. But as news of defeat had spread to everywhere, the officials in the various places wanted to protect themselves. None of them brought their armies to the capital to defend the emperor.

On the fourth day of the third month, the emperor called the court officials to a conference. Someone suggested to move the capital back to Nanjing,

The tablet stands on a pedestal of carved stone.

but Zhu Youjian could not make up his mind. On the sixth day, the insurgent army occupied Xuanfu, an important town north of Beijing. When the insurgent army reached the Juyong Pass of the Great Wall on the fifteenth day, Tang Tong, the Marquis of Dingxi, who had been awarded with a great red robe by the emperor seven days before, and Du Zhizhi, a eunuch of the Department of Rites, surrendered and opened the gate. The insurgent army was able to drive straight on and encircled Beijing in a tight cordon.

On the 16th day, the emperor called the court officials to a conference again. With tears brimming in their eyes, the emperor and officials could not find a way out of the emergency. They sighed mournfully and dispersed.

On the 18th day, Li Zicheng set up his command post outside the Zhangyi Gate (today's Guangan Gate) of the city. Du Xun, a eunuch, brought a verbal message from Li Zicheng to the emperor. He urged the emperor to "take care of himself" and flee. Shen Xiuzhi, a eunuch guarding the imperial tombs tried to persuade the emperor to abdicate. The emperor was in a dilemma and could not make a decision. Early, he had hoped that Wu Sangui, the defending general at the Shanhai Pass, might bring his army south and come to his aide. But it was too late now. At about six p.m. on that day, the Zhangyi Gate was suddenly opened. It was a signal given by Cao Huachun, the eunuch, to welcome Li Zicheng's insurgent army into the city. Then, one after another, all the gates of the inner city and outer city fell into enemy hands.

The palace was now in chaotic confusion. Zhu Youjian sent men to take his three sons separately to hide in the houses of their relatives and then ordered Empress Zhou to commit suicide. When Honorable

Five stone sacrificial vessels.

Imperial Concubine Yuan tried to hang herself, the rope broke. Zhu Youjian slashed her shoulder with his sword. He summoned the 15-year-old princess to him and cut off her left arm and then wounded several more of his concubines. He was on the verge of becoming mentally deranged.

It was already midnight. The emperor looked left and right and found only Wang Chengen, a eunuch and Commander of the City Garrison, at his side. After drinking several cups of wine, the two changed into ordinary clothes and hats, armed themselves with three-barreled guns and rode on horseback out of the Eastern Flowery Gate to the Chaoyang Gate. They falsely claimed that Wang was sent by the emperor to go out of the city. But the defending Ming army on the gate tower said they had to wait until daylight to check their identity. They tried to force their way out, but the soldiers on the gate tower fired their guns. They then turned north and came to the Anding Gate. There were no defenders there, but "the gate was tightly closed and could not be opened." After losing all hope of going out of the city, they had no alternative but to return to the palace. It was already time to hold the morning court. They struck the bell, but on court officials came. Seeing no way out, the emperor, accompanied by Wang Chengen, came to the Huangshou Pavilion on the Longevity Hill behind the palace and hanged himself at daybreak. It was the morning of the 19th day of the third month, the beginning of another day.

The Emperor's Three Sons Attend His Funeral; The Last Emperor Is Buried in a Concubine's Tomb.

At daybreak on the 19th day of the third month in the 17th year of Chongzhen (1644), Wang Xiangyao, the city defending eunuch, opened the city's Xuanwu Gate and surrendered. The insurgent army rushed into the imperial city and palace and searched everywhere for Zhu Youjian but could not find him. He was found on the following day dressed in a blue robe with a boot on one foot and the other foot was bare. Written in ink on the front of his robe were his last words, in which he still blamed the fall of the Ming dynasty on the officials, saying "The officials have failed me." There were also some words on the side, which read: "All the officials are to go to the Eastern Palace for action." Even before his death, Zhu Youjian still held out a faint hope for reviving his dynasty.

The insurgent army put Zhu Youjian and Empress Zhou in coffins of willow wood, placed them outside the Eastern Flowery Gate of the palace and allowed Ming officials to pay their last respects. His three sons (the 16-year-old eldest son, 14-year-old third son and 10-year-old fourth son) were brought to the coffins of their parents to perform kowtow rituals. On the 23rd day, the insurgent army took the coffins to Changping and left after leaving them at the foot of the Changping city wall. The treasury of Changping Prefecture was empty at the time. Xu Zuomei, the funeral overseer and a former senior official of the Board of Rites, collected donations from some Ming officials. The copper coins he collected amounted to 350 strings of cash, or 230 ounces of silver. With this money, he found some laborers to have the tomb of Honorable Imperial Concubine Tian opened and buried Zhu Youjian and Empress Zhou in it on the fourth day of the fourth month.

Honorable Imperial Concubine Tian was born in Yangzhou and married the Prince of Xin in the seventh year of Tianqi (1627). Much favored by the future emperor, she was given the title of imperial concubine a year later. A eunuch recalled, "The imperial concubine was a person of few words but of considerable talent." After giving birth to the emperor's fifth and sixth sons, she was conferred the title of Honorable Imperial Concubine.

In the 13th or 14th year of Chongzhen, the eunuch Cao Huachun brought several sing-song women from the south. When Zhu Youjian became very close with them, Tian wrote a poem admonishing the emperor. The emperor became very displeased and said sarcastically to her, "I haven't seen you for several months. Your learning seems to have improved. There were song and dance performances during all the previous reigns. I didn't start them." From then on, he refused to see her for three months. But later, Zhu Youjian seemed to have realized that he had been overdoing it. The two then became reconciled.

Tian died of illness in the seventh month of the 15th year of Chongzhen (1642) when she was 31, and was buried in a tomb in the Heavenly Longevity Mountain tomb area. In the first month of the 17th year (1644), she was reburied at a grand funeral.

To win the support of Han scholars and officials, the Great Qing dynasty, after establishing its capital in Beijing, reburied the three of them in a tomb and enlarged it to the size of an emperor's tomb, which became known as Siling.

The Ming dynasty of the Zhu family thus came to an end after 272 years of reign (1368-1644). It was the year of the Monkey. As a common saying goes, "When the tree falls, the monkeys disperse." When the big tree that was the emperor fell, the civil and military officials who followed him here and there dispersed, each planning for his own future.

Stone tablet marking the grave of Wang Chengen, eunuch and Commander of the City Garrison.

图书在版编目（CIP）数据

明十三陵帝后妃嫔轶闻／兰佩瑾策划；魏玉清编著；朱力摄影．
－北京：外文出版社，2007

ISBN 978－7－119－05114－7

Ⅰ．明… Ⅱ．①兰…②魏…③朱… Ⅲ．①十三陵－图集②帝王－故事
－中国－明代－英文③后妃－故事－中国－明代－英文 Ⅳ．K928.76－64
K827＝48 K828.5

中国版本图书馆 CIP 数据核字(2007)第 149152 号

策　　　划：兰佩瑾
编　　　著：魏玉清
摄　　　影：朱　力　等
翻　　　译：汤博文　等
设　　　计：元　青　等
责 任 编 辑：兰佩瑾

明十三陵帝后妃嫔轶闻

© 外文出版社
外文出版社出版
（中国北京百万庄大街 24 号）
邮政编码：100037
外文出版社网页：http://www.flp.com.cn
外文出版社电子邮件地址：info@flp.com.cn
sales@flp.com.cn
北京外文印刷厂印刷
中国国际图书贸易总公司发行
（中国北京车公庄西路 35 号）
北京邮政信箱第 399 号　邮政编码 100044
2008 年(小 16 开)第 1 版
2008 年第 1 版第 1 次印刷
（英）
ISBN 978－7－119－05114－7
08000（平）
85－E－660P